Calling all Authors

A *Seriously Useful* Authors Guide to Becoming a Successful Author

Mary Cavanagh

To Gina

With best wishes

Mary

New Generation Publishing

Everything the author of fiction and non-fiction needs to know about:

Publishing Methods: Mainstream, Self- Publishing and eBooks

Manuscript Presentation

Approaching Publishers and Literary Agents

Producing an eBook

Understanding The Book Industry and Bookshops

Publicity and Marketing: How To Sell That Book!

Social Media: Twitter and Facebook etc. for Marketing

Calling All Authors really has to be *the* most detailed, informative, and insightful guide for authors on the market.

Caro Fraser, London, 2015.
Author of the renowned Caper Court series

Introduction

Calling All Authors is aimed at everyone who writes fiction or non-fiction, including the established author, the self-published, the eBookers, and those of you who are still fighting your way through the options of seeing your work in print.

I undertook to write this book because I wanted to produce a valuable insight into the publishing industry – and your options within it – as seen by an ordinary working author of fiction, struggling to make sales in a marketplace that has changed out of all recognition in the last five years. Over many years I've been mainstream published (with three houses), self-published (both paperback and eBook), written two editions of this current self-help book, and co-written an acclaimed series of anthologies (the Oxford Stories). Although I've had a great deal of experience and personal success I've also been subjected to disappointments and let-downs. Thus, I will try to advise you on how to deal with the publishing industry.

I'm not a professional publicist, nor a journalist, and have no influential contacts or work experience in the publishing industry. Neither am I wealthy, young and beautiful, well connected socially, or with a far-reaching network of career and leisure contacts to boost my sales. Had I not put my shoulder to the wheel it's doubtful I'd have made many sales at all! I call myself a kitchen table author: hard-working, ambitious, dedicated to my craft and determined to use any opportunity to the best effect. So many self-help books on the subject have been written from a corporate or theoretical point of view, and not by someone like me who has pounded the pavements, and spent hours on the computer, trying to devise unique ploys to get my books 'talked up'.

The original version of this book was published as *A Seriously Useful Authors Guide to Marketing and Publicising Books* in 2009, and in the following six short years, the publishing world has turned on its head. The industry, at all levels, is now experiencing a cut-throat desperation to make a profit and survive. Why? Lots of reasons. The bite of the economic downturn started the ball rolling, and many well-known companies and imprints were forced out of business. Some very worthy and well-respected ones survive, but some, although calling themselves leaner and fitter, only do so by very close profit margins, and so often seek a quick turn round of sales by publishing 'the celebrity author'. Whilst it's true that sex sells everything, the second contender must be the 'celebrity' factor; so often a Z-lister, scooped up from current popularity, and exploited while their fleeting presence survives. This means that professional career authors find they have to compete for publicity attention. I know this must sound like sour grapes, but the market is swamped with biographies, comedy stuff, cookery books, and show-biz novelists, with accompanying scepticism that the actual 'name' has put very little blood, sweat and tears into the production – unlike writers of integrity and talent who take a pride in their work. Us!

Now, more than ever, we have to stand right at the back of the queue, alongside (and this may surprise you) many established household names who are told to *'get off your backsides and get out there'* to make sales. Thus, the advice and guidance I've included is aimed at a very large crowd indeed.

Calling All Authors also includes valuable pre-publication advice. You all want the quality of your book to be presented in a first class way, so I will attempt to lead you through the essential stages of manuscript preparation. In addition I've included the state of mainstream publishing, approaching literary agents, and looking at why many people are considering self-publishing, both paper print and eBooks. I've also explained the many stages your manuscript goes through, from the completed computer version you send off as an attachment, to seeing the finished product appear. A complicated process!

The 'explosion' of the eBook has become a very important part of the industry and is here to stay, so there is a fully dedicated section, from getting one 'put up there' to the profits you're likely to make. This part of the industry has very different publicity and marketing methods to that of paper versions, and thus, I've included the help and advice of five eBook authors who have proved to be successful.

This leads on nicely to the most significant change in the marketing and publicity of books in the last five years; the huge explosion of social media networking, such as Facebook and Twitter.

Inevitably, some of you will already have some knowledge of the publishing world, but in order to encompass those who don't, the content will be fully comprehensive and simplified. I've aimed to produce a 'grass-roots' handbook, catering for a range people from those who know absolutely nothing, to those who have had some initial experience. The aim is that *Calling All Authors* will be chock full of seriously useful information that will help you to become a successful author. I make no false promises that the advice given will catapult your book into the national bestseller lists, or turn you into a household name. Not everything will work first time, and some things *never* work, no matter how many times you try. Yes –we all hear about a mega-selling sensation that has appeared 'out of nowhere', or an eBook that has 'gone viral', but it's a rare occurrence. You may be surprised to hear that only 5% of mainstream published books sell over three thousand copies, and if some of the residual 95% only sell a few hundred they feel incredibly pleased. The reasons for this? As already mentioned, the largest proportion of publishers marketing budgets are allocated to a tiny handful of their most famous authors, and thus, the market place is saturated with both first time and lesser-known authors, all fighting to get their heads above the parapet. With these statistics you might be better to self-publish and much more on this will be comprehensively detailed. With either method your job is to work hard, to create a reputation for your book, and hope it'll be *the one* that goes that extra mile.

I must repeat that I can't promise you instant success – some things that work well for one person will fall flat for another – and you have to get used to the 'custard pie' treatment. However, if you truly believe in your book you stand a very good chance of succeeding, and books that have active authors behind them do substantially better than those that don't.

I hope you find my book lively, highly readable, and very useful. Please do *not* skip any of the chapters you might think are irrelevant, as a great deal of it will apply to your manuscript production, and knowledge of the book trade. In trying to 'make it' as an author you'll need energy, innovation, commitment and a very thick skin, so I will conclude with my own personal mantra:

If you want to succeed you must never say, 'I can't be bothered'! You must always be bothered, even when you're tired, demoralised and pig sick of the whole thing.

Good Luck to you all. And more than anything, enjoy yourselves.

Foreword

By Caro Fraser
Author of the renowned Caper Court Series

After sixteen successful years as a published author, during which time I wrote six of the *Caper Court* novels (a series set in a barristers' chambers) and six stand-alone novels, my sales had always been pleasingly constant. I had a solid fan following, but suddenly, due to the failure of my publisher's new automated distribution system, my sales figures (and those of a number of other mid-list authors) took a dip. This resulted in my agent finding it hard to find a publisher for my seventh Caper Court book, *Breath of Corruption*. I knew from the hundreds of emails coming into my website that there was an enthusiastic market for the book, so instead of shelving it, I decided to self-publish.

I took on the services of a self-publishing company who offered an excellent package, covering everything from proofreading to production and distribution, as well as a comprehensive marketing service. However, despite this service and support, it still left me with a lot of work to do to sell my book. The more I looked into being my own publicity and marketing manager, the more daunting a task it seemed. There were so many aspects to be considered, from organising a launch, getting reviews, persuading bookshops and libraries to stock it, and generally getting it talked up in many areas only known to those with experience.

Having had no previous need to consider self-marketing, I realised I had to find some focused help. I put up a request via my website for any guidance, and that's how I met Mary Cavanagh. She had a wealth of knowledge at her fingertips, through marketing her excellent debut mainstream novel, *The Crowded Bed*, and self-publishing the Oxford Stories anthologies, and was the ideal person to guide me through the process.

Self-publishing *Breath of Corruption* opened up a whole new world to me. Not only was Mary able to show me exactly what was needed to make sales, and the processes involved, she demonstrated, through her enthusiasm and her love of writing, that while self-publicity might be hard work, it can be an immensely rewarding and sociable experience.

I decided that her advice was too useful to keep to myself, so with her agreement I posted a series of her articles on my blog site, to help both published and self-published authors. She wrote from first hand practical experience, not only offering all kinds of tips and constructive ideas, but wise words on the highs and lows of the procedure. I really learned something about what goes on behind the scenes of the book trade as well.

There were so many topics involved it quickly became apparent that the material would be put to much better use, and reach a far wider audience, in the form of a self-help book. This updated version of the original book, now entitled *Calling All Authors,* is the result.

To conclude. The work I put into my self-published book was not wasted, as it resulted in a contract with a mainstream publisher for the next book in the Caper Court series. However, like Mary, I find that the world of publicity and marketing has seriously changed, and I too, have to get my head around 'internet selling'; something that doesn't come naturally.

Mary's writing is clear, concise, and encouraging, and includes so many innovative ideas, and the sort of useful contacts that can only be found through hands-on experience. *Calling All Authors* really has to be *the* most detailed, informative, and insightful guide for authors on the market.

Caro Fraser
London 2015

www.caro-fraser.com

The Contents

Part Five:

The Importance of Sales Campaign

Part Six:

Those All Important Reviews 87

Part Ten:

Marketing and Publicity: It's Time To Go Out and Hand Sell That Book 139

Current publications by

Mary Cavanagh

Novels:
The Crowded Bed – Transita 2007
The Priest, His Lady and The Drowned Child – Thames River Press, 2013
Who Was Angela Zendalic – Thames River Press, 2014

eBooks:
The Crowded Bed – Oxford eBooks, 2015
The Priest, His Lady and The Drowned Child – Oxford eBooks, 2015
Who Was Angela Zendalic – Oxford eBooks, 2015

Self-help Books for Authors:
A Seriously Useful Guide to Marketing and Publicising Books – Troubador 2009
Calling All Authors – OxPens/New Generation Publishing, 2015.

OxPens Anthologies:
Published by OxPens with the Oxford Writers Group:
The Sixpenny Debt and Other Oxford Stories
The Lost College and Other Oxford Stories
The Bodleian Murders and Other Oxford Stories

About Mary

Mary lives in Kennington, a large village near Oxford, with her husband Bill, and their wire-haired Dachshund, Lovejoy. She spent her childhood in the mellow, leafy climes of North Oxford, and attended St Barnabas Junior School in Jericho; a privilege she feels honoured to have shared with such friendly and unpretentious classmates. Milham Ford Girls Grammar was another story. Being lazy, and academically challenged, she was grateful to show a clean pair of heels. A working life of sorts followed, with a range of diverse jobs, none of which she took at all seriously. After marriage and two sons, she became a mature student at Westminster Teacher Training College (now part of Oxford Brookes University). Whilst always being a voracious reader it was through her English course that she discovered the joy of creative writing.

She describes her work as strong contemporary fiction, born out of her observations and experiences, most especially as a voyeur of 'humankind' and an ardent 'earwigger'. She is also fascinated with the strange and secret life that's lived within the mind, man's battle with close relationships, and the profound changes, both social and moral, that have taken place in her lifetime.

Her work has been compared to Susan Hill, Henry Fielding, Virginia Woolf, Joanna Trollope, Anita Shreve, and Pat Barker. (What a diverse list!) Her own most admired writers are Kate Atkinson, Monica Dickens, Arnold Bennet, and the prose writing of Ian McEwan.

She is a member of the Oxford Writers Group (OWG) and Writers in Oxford,
Website: http://:marycavanagh.co.uk
Email: mary.cavanagh20@gmail.com

Acknowledgments

Whilst writing this book I contacted a great many people involved in the publishing industry, searching for the latest tips, anecdotes, and general help. I was stunned by the overwhelming and enthusiastic responses I received. Some of them even offered to be interviewed, or to submit articles, and I was delighted to accept. *Calling All Authors* is, therefore, most definitely a joint effort, and so much the richer for it. I'm very grateful to the following people for their time and generosity.

The renowned author, Caro Fraser, for her enthusiastic and supportive foreword.
Andy Severn, the eBook Publisher, director of Oxford eBooks.
Jo Barton, the Book Blogger, from *Jaffareadstoo.*
Lynne Moores, the Library Service Manager.
The contributing authors: Angela Cecil Reid, Polly Courtney, Alice Jolly, John Kitchen, Marissa de Luna, Debrah Martin and Tim Stevens.
Also, my three author contributors who requested to remain anonymous.

Mary Cavanagh
Oxford 2015
http//:marycavanagh.co.uk

Part One:

Your Journey To Publication

Chapter 1 : The Loneliness of the Long Distance Author

On Being an Author

Are you an author of fiction or non-fiction who, as yet, is unpublished and investigating the future of your work? Do you want a mainstream contract? Are you thinking about self-publishing? Are you interested in the eBook market? Have you been mainstream published in the past and are now considering other options? If you are any of these then I'm sure you'll benefit from the advice, guidance, and tips this valuable self-help book contains, no matter what your current stage.

Fact. To be a successful author you first need to be an avaricious and eclectic reader, and that doesn't mean you have to have any professional literary qualifications. Far from it. The novelists amongst you are inspired to create in the same way as your most admired authors, and every one of you has a burning desire to become a 'bestselling' author, too. For writers of non-fiction, and this may surprise you, you also need parallel skills to invent and create your work into a flowing and absorbing prose. Topics can range from historical research, business, travel, life-skills, or a 'How-To' book, and must be written with flair and energy in order to engage your reader.

Anyone with a lively imagination can pick up a pen, but you really *do* need to have absorbed as much about the literary world as possible, to be inspired and to know where your own work 'sits' in the industry. You also write because you want to produce an excellent work that will be admired, and my little joke is that everyone who starts to write is inwardly rehearsing a major prize winners speech. I can remember how excited I was when I first began – spending every spare moment writing, and all other headspace thinking about my plot and characters. I'd even wake up in the night and scribble down an idea, only to find that in the morning I couldn't make any sense of it! However, if you're serious about completing a work, there's no other way to do it other than to become wholly focussed and absorbed. You become so wrapped up in the creative process your family and friends might comment that you seem to be in another world (and of course, you are). It doesn't matter if they think you're mad, deluded, or just plain selfish. This is what you want to do and most writers, especially those with complex demands, have to seriously rearrange their lives to find time to write. Some work far into the night, and some get up well before dawn to get a few hours in before the family takes over.

Belonging To A Writing Group

Belonging to a writing group can provide invaluable support. You form a bond with the like-minded, and have a chance to read pieces of your work to a friendly, receptive audience. In return, you'll get valuable constructive feedback and benefit from the networking that goes on within the writing world. If you already belong to one you'll know of the advantages, but if not, and you can't find one, then initially ask in your main library, or local bookshops, for one to contact. Many have waiting lists, so if you can't wait then why not start one yourself – again contact the library or bookshop and see if you can put up an advertisement.

The possible downside of a writing group might be that its management is unstructured. You'll need at least three people at the helm to act as chair, secretary, and treasurer, but with the wants and needs of a diverse group, they need to be diplomatic and constant in attendance. My own, The Oxford Writers Group, also has a committee, formed of the three post holders and a couple of others. The committee is given the brief to form key decisions, and to implement the (never used so far) grievance policy. A second problem could be that some members constantly hog their allotted time and need to be reined in, and a third that it drives you nuts having to listen to other members work in a genre in which you have no interest. If this is the case then remember that they might feel the same about yours!

The Value of Writing Courses

The range of people who set out to write are very variable in confidence. Those who have modest self-belief they can do it, others who are so diffident they're afraid to talk about 'their secret' with anyone, and some, dare I say it, who overvalue their abilities. No matter what type you are, the usefulness of a structured writing course will prove to be invaluable. These can range from those run by local education (less these days due to the usual cuts) academic departments in the University cities, residential organisations such as Arvon, or distance learning online. For those with ambition you can even take a degree in Creative Writing. Prices can vary, and none are actually 'cheap', but it'll be a wise investment – not just for the quality of your writing but by introducing you to a network of support. When I started my first novel I joined a group run by Oxford's Continuing Education Department and it was quite invaluable. I met a group of energetic, talented people, many of whom I still keep in touch with, and my writing standard advanced considerably.

Joining an Internet Support Group

Another encouragement is to join an online writing support group, most especially in the stages leading up to publication. The following article is from Angela Cecil Reid, a children's writer and biographer, and a fellow member of the Oxford Writers' Group. Here she talks about the value of belonging to Internet Support Groups.

The Value of Internet Support Groups, by Angela Cecil Reid

For aspiring writers one of the most useful resources is the internet, and websites connected with writing abound. They offer advice on technique, how to get published, lists of publishers, and agents as well as offering competitions and access to groups who will critique your work. While this can be invaluable for the novice writer, who does not have access to a local writers' group, it is also useful for the more experienced writer by providing an anonymous way of trying out material.

One of the largest and most popular sites of my experience is YouWriteOn (www.youwriteon.com). This site was funded by the Arts Council in 2006 and soon had over 10,000 members. Unlike some sites, which rely on the fact that their members have paid a subscription to keep them involved, YouWriteOn has developed a system of reading credits whereby work is submitted (usually, but not always, the opening chapters of a novel, or a short story) and is initially reviewed 'for free'. However, for further reviews, you have to achieve Reading Credits by reading and critiquing other people's work which is selected for you at random. There is also a points system, which the reviewer uses to rate the piece they are critiquing, and test questions to make sure they have actually read the piece in the first place. The year is now split into six 'development' months and six 'editorial critique competition' months. The rating system results in a 'top ten' of the most highly rated pieces in each 'development' month, and a number of the most promising entries are selected for a free critique by an editor from Orion or Random House during the 'competition' months. Highly rated chapters are also added to 'The Bestsellers Chart'. The opening chapters of *Nile Cat,* my own novel for children and young teens, reached this chart, which I found most encouraging.

Other websites may charge a subscription and work in a different way. Write Words (www.writewords.org.uk) for example, is a subscription site. It is made up of a lively community of writers offering articles, interviews with published authors, and forums for discussing all things connected with writing and being published. Here you join a small group of writers who are all working in your chosen genre and as a result you get to know each other's work well, and not just the opening chapters as on YouWriteOn. You also have the ability to set the privacy levels on your work and can choose whether any visitor to the website, Write Words members, or even just your group, can read it. The groups cover genres from journalism to science fiction and memoir to all types of fiction. Some are more active than others – so be selective and be prepared – as there can be a waiting list for the most popular groups.

Another popular website is *authonomy,* (www.authonomy.com) conceived and managed by editors at HarperCollins Publishers. It is an online community set up with the aim of connecting readers, writers, and publishing professionals. *authonomy* invites writers to post their manuscripts, complete or unfinished, on the website. Authors create their own personal page to host their project and members can rate and comment on these submissions – and importantly can personally recommend their favourites to the community. *authonomy* uses the activity of its members to rank books on the site. It costs nothing to create a profile, to upload your book, or to read and recommend the books on offer. The intention is that the community will guide publishers straight to the freshest writing talent. HarperCollins states its aim is to find new, talented writers to sign up for their traditional book publishing programme; they read the most popular manuscripts each month as part of this ongoing search for talent.

A common factor of all writing websites is that to get the most out of them, you have to invest time. You may be posting to a forum to raise your profile, offering or receiving advice, or reviewing other people's writing. The latter is particularly useful as analysing what works and does not work in other peoples' chapters, and will assist you in developing your own writing skills. Having your own work critiqued, even with varying levels of skill, is also most helpful; it can raise self-confidence, and while all critiques are supposed to be constructive, rather than negative, they can give the first valuable lessons in coping with rejection. Generally the more active, and diplomatic you are, on any website, the better your own book will do.

Chapter 2 : Quality Control

How Does Your Manuscript Compare to Professional Standards?

Success as an author has always been difficult, but over the last few years the complex changes in the book industry means that triumph can be judged in many different ways. New vistas have opened up alongside the conventional mainstream deal, so those with self-published books, or eBooks, can have their own large fan bases. However, success in any area will depend on *you*, and the more you do in the pre-publication stage the bigger chance you have to achieve your goal. No matter what method you choose it's essential that your manuscript is professional and well produced, so the next section involves quality control.

All authors love the writing process. You sit crouched over your computer, tablet, or writing pad, producing hundred (even thousands) of words a day, in a stream of creativity. You live entirely enclosed in your plot, characters, or subject matter. You constantly read your work back to yourself, to add, subtract, cut and paste, and consult your dictionary and thesaurus to find exactly the right word or nuance. Of course there are days when you suffer from 'writers block', or you're exhausted by the demands of work and family – that's all part of being a writer – but on the whole it's a hugely enjoyable process. Then, after many months, or even years, the day comes when you've finished your *magnum opus.* But here is the cautionary tale; your manuscript will be far from ready. The creative process is over and serious editing must begin.

All ambitious writers are driven and enthusiastic, with a huge impetus of invention. No one sets out to produce a flawed manuscript, but it's a miserable fact that you probably have, and thus quality control applies to everyone. A highly creative novelist can actually 'fall in love' with their work, and like every star-crossed lover become blind to its flaws. Writers of non-fiction are sometimes so eager to present their factual knowledge that they fail to present good, entertaining prose. In fact, some of the most creative brains in the world can produce a dodgy manuscript, and although everyone says, 'that can't be me', then eat some humble pie and take a step back.

In trying to get your work published you have a choice; trying to secure a mainstream publishing contract or going down the self-publishing/eBook route. Each method has its advantages and disadvantages, all discussed later, but the minute your book goes out to public scrutiny you'll be competing in a huge, highly critical market. Thus, your writing has to stand up to the yardstick of existing professionals and whilst varying standards of prose exist, there's no room in the industry for a second-rate presentation. With Amazon, and other feedback sites, you'll be at the mercy of bad reviews, and the horror of Internet 'trolls' who make it their life's work to be spiteful and scathing. If you're applying to a literary agent, you'll want a pristine presentation, or if 'going it alone' you won't want to run the risk of your work being totally panned in this way. It'll only end up as a huge embarrassment to carry around for the rest of your career.

One example (of course, there's no naming of names) concerns a self-published book that was (through huge good luck), taken up by a large publishing house and consequently sold thousands. The story was ingenious, and a real page-turner, but ten per cent of the reviews on Amazon were 'one star', all commenting on the poor editing and incredibly bad standard of grammar, and it beats me why the publishing house didn't think it necessary to revalue it. You may think, 'so what'. 90% of the reviews were good enough, it made alot of money for the author, and he or she went on to have their second and third books snapped up by a ready-made audience. Yes – that's likely to be the case – but does *any* author want to have the sneer of derision hanging onto their coat tails?

Editing and Perfecting Your Manuscript

The biggest failing of inexperienced authors is that they're so close up to their work they can fail to pick up simple mistakes, or even gross 'howlers'. After a quick whizz through a computer spell and grammar check you might think that it seems in pretty good order, but it's not enough, by a long chalk, to ensure perfection. This is the advice I give, based on my own experiences.

1. Initially, use the standard spell/grammar checker found on your computer, ensuring you address punctuation and spacing between words. Once completed there are many other processes to go through. If you use compound words, such as *they've, don't, I'll* and *I'm*, use 'find and replace' to check if they're used in the way you wish, and conjoined words need to be looked up in a good dictionary. For instance, is it, text book, text-book or textbook? Is it middle men, middle-men or middlemen? I've actually found it's easier to look up the words using an online Oxford dictionary than heave out my extremely heavy copy. If you've changed the name of a character along the way (a common practice) put both names through the 'find and replace' feature, to check all is regular. I've been caught out myself with this and it's infuriating.

2. Next, read the completed manuscript on your computer screen by changing the *size and the font* so you're psychologically tricked into reading what looks like a 'new work'. I type my manuscripts

with Verdana 14 point, so I always change it to the clarity and increased size of Arial 18 point. You'll be amazed at what horrors you turn up. You can read the same sentence so many times you fail to notice errors or missing words, and also check every few paragraphs for repeated adjectives or verbs. Ensure your speech marks and full stops are all there, that every paragraph has an indent, and your section breaks are in place.

3. Then 'right justify' the manuscript and print it out in your choice of a readable font – yes, the full work – and read it through *carefully*. Believe me, what looks good on a screen can come out seriously wrong on paper. Then slowly read every page aloud to yourself, as if you're auditioning for a play, to ensure that the end result 'sounds' right. Again, you'll be amazed at how many more errors you turn up. It's really hard work, and you can end up getting quite punch drunk, but don't rush it. When your book is produced, and you discover even the tiniest error (and I've had to beat myself up on many an occasion), you'll be furious with yourself.

Factual Correctness

Both fiction and non-fiction writers must take care when editing for factual correctness and anachronistic errors. I once piled six adults, plus their luggage and a dog, into a two-seater Lagonda sports car! If you mention retail products, shops, architecture, geographical areas, food, artefacts, politics, or music of any era, check your facts are correct. If you write *anything* about the past don't be lazy and rely on memory or anecdotes. Look it up! The modern wonder of Google means that it's not the slog it used to be, with library visits and endless searching of textbooks. Remember! If you don't get it right the 'trolls' will take a huge delight in nitpicking to find fault; much better to spend time on your manuscript than have your book publically slated by an anonymous coward. In my first novel, *The Crowded Bed,* I stated the wrong day of a Jewish baby's circumcision, and received a vicious letter setting me straight! So the moral is, if you don't take supreme care, bad editing could end up as a huge embarrassment, and haunt you for the rest of your career.

Also, make sure than any text you use from other sources are 'allowed' under copyright. In reproducing extracts from other works of literature and poetry it depends on the age of the piece, and as far as I can find out (it's complicated!) one hundred years since publication is the minimum. If you want to quote song lyrics there are even more complicated rules, involving applying for time-consuming 'permissions'. However, I've been told that using a couple of lines won't ruffle any feathers.

Professional Proofreading or Copy Editing
If you're still feeling a little diffident, even after a meticulous self-edit, you might be interested in using one of the many firms that offer a professional editing service. Firms charge by the hour or the page, so you would need to get a personal quote for either proofreading or copy-editing. Proofreading covers spelling, punctuation and grammar, and copy-editing will do all of the above, plus evaluate the quality of the text, and flag up any weak areas. They should also check for plagiarism and copyright permissions.

Whole Manuscript Assessment
Another service on offer is manuscript assessment. This is a detailed and comprehensive written report on how your book stands up to professional competition, and advises as to whether you might have a chance of a mainstream contract. Here they tend to charge by the page, so you'll

agree a fixed price for the service. It can be expensive. The average for an 85,000 word novel would be £600-£700 (Summer 2015). In choosing one you'll have to wade through all the options found online, or advertised in specialised Writers Magazines. Even better if a fellow writer can recommend a good one, but always make sure they have positive testimonials and several genuine 'success stories'. Many of the better firms list their editors and their backgrounds, and as they're usually authors and ex-editors try to get someone who is *au fait* with your genre of writing, or knows exactly where your novel, historical text or information book, 'sits' in the open market. Do you write for children, or the Young Adult market? If so, you should immediately turn into these pathways and investigate the various categories. Do you write crime, romance, clogs and shawls, fantasy, vampires, ghosts and ghoulies, historical fiction, chic-lit or erotica? Crime can be anything from cosy crime, similar to Miss Marple, or gangland massacres. Romance, can range from Mills and Boon (a highly popular market) to literary works like *Wuthering Heights*. If your writing is indefinable, but includes many aspects of the above, the term 'commercial fiction' is usually the one that applies. Deep literary fiction, of the sort that concentrates on beautiful prose, also has its followers, but your writing must be accompanied by a good plot and well-drawn characters to stand any chance. One brilliant writer I know has never had any success, due to the fact that his haughty retort to advice was, 'Plot! What plot?'

Most of the well-established firms will offer an excellent standard of service, and can be relied upon to give you a constructive report, but at the same time they might be critical. After all, that's why you're paying them, and they could suggest partial re-writes, or changing an aspect of your storyline. Initially, you might be taken aback – as if they're accusing your baby of being ugly – but they're merely pointing out where certain weaknesses lie, and shouldn't be dismissed out of hand. However, at the end of the day, it's your work and if you think they're wrong you have the right to ignore advice.

On the positive side they may state they have links to literary agents, and will recommend your work if they think it's good enough. This is a huge incentive, and I know of some cases where this has happened, so if you find you're one of the chosen ones it'll be a valuable 'in' well ahead of the queue.

So. After all editing options have been covered, and your manuscript is in the best and finest order possible, it's time to try to get it published. You now have three choices, in no particular order of preference.

    a.   Try to secure a mainstream publishing contract.

    b.   Approach a publishing company who will take 'unsolicited manuscripts' directly from the author.

    c.   Self Publish (Hardback, Paperback, or eBook)

Part Two:

Mainstream Publishing Houses

Chapter 3 : We All Want A Mainstream Contract (Or Do We?)

How Mainstream Operates

This is where the author signs a contract with an established publishing house, and might (rare these days) receive an advance on future receipts. Fiction writers will need to have fully completed their work, but non-fiction writers are, I believe, advised to pitch an idea to a publishing company before actually completing the book.

All contracts within the industry are fairly standard, but you would be wise to spend a great deal of time on the legalese so you fully understand exactly what you're signing up to. There should be no financial input and you will receive an agreed percentage of 'royalty', which is your percentage of the *net* receipts on sales, currently around 7%/8%. This means your cut is calculated on the price the publishing house receives per copy, and with there being no retail price index rule these days huge discounts are negotiated by various middlemen (more of them later). A ballpark figure will be that you receive between 25 pence and 30 pence a book, so you can easily work out that unless you sell huge amounts, or the film rights, it's never going to be a money-spinner. However, it's still what most authors want – to be part of an established, professional set-up. The upside is that no financial risk is involved, and all editing and production costs are the responsibility of the publisher. However, also note that you'll have no control over the production or the timeline, and you'll sign away your 'rights' for a set period. Here I will differentiate between copyright and rights. Every word you write is legally protected in law as your *copyright.* This means it's an offence for anyone to pass it off as their own, or reproduce it without your permission. *Rights* are what you sign away as part of the standard contract, which gives your publisher the 'right' to publish or sell your work in *other forms*, such as audio, large print, foreign deals, translations and film rights. If a contract between a publisher and an author comes to an end for any reason, your rights should be returned to you within a specified period.

It takes a publishing house quite a long time to produce the book for sale after you've signed up – anything up to a year – but well before the publication date you should be appointed an in-house editor to work with you. They will have been picked for having a good knowledge of the market your book is aimed at, will have a good literary knowledge, and be briefed to ensure the content is presented in an exemplary way. Although your work will have already gone through your own careful presentation, and the publishers will have assessed it 'in-house' before the contract is signed, they will apply their own further criteria. This may result in you being asked to do some re-writing, but all mainstream productions will have gone through this process, even those written by the most famous authors with long histories of success. The upside is that you'll be able to get to know your editor, and it would be wise, initially, to listen. You'll usually have the chance to argue your case, and that could lead to a compromise. Try to keep a pragmatic balance, and don't ever take things personally. The thing to remember is that the publishing world is a business and he/she is trying to produce a book that will avoid criticism and can go on to sell many copies.

The cover design process will involve the entire production team to ensure market appeal. Some publishers might allow you to comment on designs, or even suggest your own ideas (rare), but part of your contract is that you place the presentation in their hands and 'they know best'. On the whole they usually have the skills to showcase a book very well, and it's rare for mistakes to happen, but one of my friends was stuck with a truly hideous, inappropriate cover. She begged her publisher to change it, and they refused, so she had no choice but to grin and bear it.

Most publishing houses boast a marketing and publicity department, but it's very difficult to generalise as to the efficacy of it. Some carry out a supreme service and some fail miserably. If you're an unknown newcomer it's unlikely they'll be ploughing much money into your campaign, but the hope is that they'll try to boost your sales and offer support in your own efforts. But don't bank on it.

Another caution: Traditionally, publishing houses would order an initial set number of books – say 500 – from a reputable printing firm, and hope to sell them. Thus, decent stock numbers were stored with wholesalers (more later) when orders came in. Now, some of the smaller ones order their books POD (Print-On-Demand) from such firms as Lightning Source. These are excellent productions of quality, but the only drawback is distribution; they might only risk small stocks, and when these have run out your orders can't be supplied until they order in again. Long delays shouldn't occur, but *they might*.

But don't let's get ahead of ourselves! In order to secure that contract it's usually the case that you'll need a literary agent. Broadly speaking it's said that it's more difficult to get a literary agent than a mainstream publisher, and believe me, it's incredibly difficult to get either.

The Role of the Literary Agent
The bottom line is that literary agents, like publishers, have to take a gamble that you can make them some money. A large agency has to show a decent profit in order to pay liveable salaries, run an office, and employ any

support staff needed. Their margin to survive, despite raking off 10-15% of your earnings, is probably very slender as most authors, even well known ones, don't sell in the large amounts they used to. Many young agents, who are currently building up their own client base, have no real income to speak of and might have to juggle another 'day job' to keep themselves afloat.

So what does an agent do? Much of their day is spent on reading manuscript submissions (the slush pile), making approaches to publishers (productive or unproductive), checking proffered contracts, fighting for the best deals possible, and looking after their clients finances. They should also find out exactly what you'll be expected to do in the publicity department, such as paying your own travel costs to bookshops and literary festivals, and funding publicity and marketing materials, such as leaflets and bookmarks. These costs might eat up all your royalty payments, so you need to know exactly where you stand.

What all agents are really looking for is an author to make them a lucrative living, such as a JK Rowling or a John Grisham, and they're always on the lookout, especially for the forerunner to a 'trend'. Such examples are *'Twilight'* by Stephenie Meyer *Fifty Shades of Grey* by E.L.James and *The Girl With The Dragon Tattoo* by Stieg Larssen. These books took off like rockets, developed into a series, and made both publishers and agents a huge amount of money. Thus, you can see why they're very selective in taking on new authors; your books need to sell, and gone are the days when publishers took on brilliant young authors and nurtured their careers towards greatness. With the industry becoming so cut-throat their authors not only have to write commercial books, but be good at going out into the market place and selling themselves with what is termed a USP – a Unique Selling Point.

How To Find a Literary Agent

In your search for a literary agent you'll probably go straight to the Internet, but my initial advice is to consult the good old-fashioned trade bible known as *The Writers and Artists Year Book* (www.writersandartists.co.uk)

In this unique production you'll find comprehensive details of agents, publishers, media publications (such as newspapers and magazines for both England and Ireland) and a large range of associated services and articles. Main libraries should stock a copy but it's really worth buying your own. All agents listed in the WAAYB belong to the Association of Authors Agents (the AAA) which is the professional body.

However, smaller agents do exist, so the Internet can be very useful in finding new, dynamic agents who are looking for clients. I Googled 'New Literary Agents' and quite a few popped up – some of them working for established firms and seeking their own clients. *The Writers Workshop* (www.writersworkshop.co.uk) also provides the excellent and comprehensive *Agent Finder*.

In selecting one to contact a 'horses for courses' rule must prevail, so make absolutely sure they take your type of work, or genre, to avoid wasted time. Whoever you contact you'll find that they generally request the same formula of an introductory letter, a brief synopsis, and three opening chapters, but always check and comply *to the letter*. Another tip is to study a chosen agent's website, and read their current section on 'submissions' just in case they're imposing 'a pause' in receiving work. Annoying as it is, it'll save you wasting your time.

Never, ever, agree to pay for any 'postal/service charges' or 'out-of-pocket' expenses as this is not the way that agents of integrity operate.

If you're taken on it's considered to be a huge coup, but this doesn't mean they'll succeed in selling your work. Some are brilliant and work tirelessly, but some seem to take you on, and then ignore you; contact with them is difficult and they can take many, many months to report back to you on progress. I've had three agents in the past, been very disappointed with every one, and will not be looking for another.

The Approach Letter

The approach letter, and the synopsis, are incredibly difficult to write. Some might say that as a writer you should have this skill at your fingertips, but it's rarely the case. It's a whole new ball game, and very few authors are natural marketing gurus. Selling yourself and your work is a really tall order, so it's worth spending a great deal of time (and frustration) in creating a pitch. Here is my own basic advice.

Don't:

Use a standard letter you've copied from an Internet advice site – they're very useful for general advice, but it needs *originality*.

Tell them how wonderful you are, inflate your personality, or show off in any way.

Use exclamation marks, flashy fonts and colours, or try to be whacky.

Tell them your friends and family think it's amazing.

Waffle on with complicated and lengthy descriptions to outline your plot.

Infer that you're a copycat of someone else, or liken yourself to someone famous.

Do:

Be professional and polite.

Make sure the agency takes work similar in genre and type to your own. Even better to single out a particular editor who you've researched and feel would like your work.

Make your introductory letter as concise as possible. Agents easily get bored and you need to get straight to the point. (I once read a very famous agent read her slush pile whilst on a running machine!)

Briefly introduce yourself, and if you have any sort of USP make sure you exploit it. Most of us don't, but try and think of *something* that makes you seem interesting and distinctive.

Show knowledge of the agency i.e. *I particularly like reading Joe Brown and/or Jenny Brown.*

Identify your target audience and say (modestly) why you think readers will enjoy the book.

Write a very short italicised paragraph to describe your work, similar to the short, enticing blurb that will go on the back cover. Fiction writers should include its genre, where it's set (geographically and in time), and a brief encapsulation of its story. Here is an example.

A story of love, fear, and drama, set in a wild part of northern England. After a troubled start in life, involving cruelty and rejection, the shy and plain orphan, Jane Eyre, becomes governess to the ward of the forbidding Mr Rochester. Thereafter her life becomes overshadowed by his austere behaviour, and the strange nocturnal happenings at Thornfield Hall. Over time Jane and Rochester fall in love, but their marriage is halted by the revelation of a horrifying secret. . .

Then, *briefly*, try to describe your plot and characters in a way that will engage their interest.

Date your letter, and ensure that something to identify you is on the footnote of every page in the tiniest font possible. (i.e.marycavanagh.co.uk - *Who Was Angela Zendalic*) as in busy offices things get separated and lost.

Use paperclips, not staples.

Writing a Synopsis

Again, this is a very hard thing to do, and although you can find many online sites that tell you how to do it, your work is so unique the only person who can get it right, is you. Agents usually request around 500 words, and in that you have to encapsulate the unique essence, quality, and magnet of your work. Excellent guidelines can be found online by Googling 'writing a synopsis' and you'll find many independent articles and literary websites, especially those of *The Literary Consultancy* (www.literaryconsultancy.co.uk) and the women's help magazine *MsLexia* (www.mslexia.co.uk). The synopsis should *not* be an intriguing enticement with lots of posed questions – all they want here is the bog standard story from start to finish. I could go on in great detail, but here are my brief tips.

Don't:

Waffle on at great length with muddled details, or give a chapter-by-chapter breakdown.

Do:

Be business-like, concise, and efficient.

Include title, author, and page numbers in the footer.

Briefly include names, ages, facets of character, and occupations of the central characters.

Tell the story *without any suspense*, but describe any 'conflict' between them.

Outline the story factually, including the end (no matter how much you want to impress the agent with 'a clever twist' or keep them guessing).

Off Goes Your Submission

If you're asked to submit by email, follow the guidelines absolutely to the letter or it'll be discarded. If you're asked for a printed paper version then include a stamped addressed postcard for receipt, and an envelope, ditto, for 'a reply'.

Once received your work will be added to the large mountain of other submissions on the 'slush pile', or the 'virtual slush pile', to wait its turn. All agents will assure you that every single one of their submissions are given full attention, but sometimes a rejection letter comes back so quickly you wonder if it's been looked at. You can only wonder! Some authors even use tricks such as placing a hair between pages, or gently dabbing the corners of pages with sugar so they stick together! Most rejection letters from agents attempt to be politely final, but if you get what's known as a genuine 'rave rejection', take heart. These short words should spur you on, and might help to interest another agent whose list is more appropriate to your type of work. However, as miserable as it is, a rejection is a rejection and you must move on. It's worth noting that J.K Rowling, John Grisham, and E.L. James were all multiple rejectees who eventually made it to the big time. If you don't hear anything back for eight weeks it's quite permissible to contact the agency and ask for progress, but be prepared for an harassed or inconclusive reply.

Before we leave agents it's worth mentioning that some agents *don't take any submissions at all*. They only rely on recommendations from the various manuscript assessment agencies (more on them later), so this narrows the field even more. I actually object to this because it means that only authors who can afford an expensive assessment stand a chance with certain agencies.

Direct Submission to a Publishing House

You may have tried to get an agent and been disappointed. You may have had your work professionally assessed and been told it will not be recommended to an agent. You may have been a very successful author in the past who has been dropped, for many reasons, by your publishing house (one friend who experienced this described it as 'the night of the long knives') and it's a truly devastating thing to happen. It's worth repeating here that many established quality authors, with active literary agents and renowned backlists, are struggling to continue to get published. The criteria seems to be, in addition to financial restraints, is that *'you're only as good as your last book'*, and if sales have dipped a bit, you can be unceremoniously axed.

The one thing left, in trying for a mainstream contract, is to approach a publisher who will receive 'unsolicited manuscripts' straight from the author. There used to be quite a few in the industry, but this number is diminishing very rapidly. I decided to phone all the UK publishing houses I thought were still accepting manuscripts directly from the author, and I asked the following:

'I am writing a self-help textbook, aimed at all authors; fiction, non-fiction, published, self-published or currently un-published. I am including a section on 'submissions'. Are you still accepting unagented manuscripts directly from authors?'

26

Some said they were sorry, but they were not. Some said that they *'didn't know'* or *'thought they still did'*, but promised to *'find out and contact me back'*. None of them did. Therefore, the list below is based on my online searches, detailing publishing houses that currently state they accept unsolicited manuscripts (Summer 2015).

Accent Press – www.accentpress.co.uk (Look under Submissions section)

Alma Books – www.almabooks.com (Look under 'contact us')

Canongate Books – www.canongate.tv (Look up Canongate Submissions) A difficult site to negotiate.

Choc-Lit – www.choc-lit.com (Look in Submissions section). A successful and well-respected publisher but with an overdetailed and rather confusing variety of submission options. I understand they like their authors to be free of literary agents.

Legend Press – www.legendtimesgroup.co.uk (Look in Submissions Section)

Myrmidon – www.myrmidonbooks.com (Look under 'contact us' for writers) Another difficult site to negotiate.

Claret Press – www.claretpress.com Not exactly a conventional small press, but extremely helpful and encouraging to a friend of mine. Best to read the website sections and decide if they would be the right one for you.

Honno Press – www.honno.co.uk - Only for women who are Welsh, living in Wales, or have a *significant* Welsh connection.

Seren Books – www.serenbooks.com (see under The Publisher – Books Submissions) Also for books connected to Wales.

Your own on-line searches might also produce some new publishers and presses.

Although I've heard of a handful of successes achieved by submitting in this way, please don't take *any* of these publishers as personal recommendations. What suits one will not suit another, and their rules may suddenly change. The certain thing is that they're all going to be swamped by hopeful authors, so you must make *absolutely sure* they accept your type of work. Their website submissions pages are very specific, and once again, I firmly advise you to follow their rules to the letter.

The point I'm making here is that, with or without a literary agent, it's incredibly difficult to get a manuscript even looked at by a publishing house, and it's all part of the painful process you have to go through if you're trying to become a mainstream published author. But don't give up!

The exciting alternative of self-publishing is open to everyone.

Part Three:

Self-Publishing a Paperback (or Hardback)

Chapter 4 : Negotiating a Maze

Your Wide Range of Options

Self-publishing is the biggest change that has taken place in the last decade. From those seeking a career as a writer, to those who wish to fulfil a showcase for their 'hobby', it's a marvellous opportunity to get your work produced in a wholly professional and attractive way. In this section you'll find a baffling amount of options, but if you slow down and investigate each one methodically, you'll be able to decide what will work for you, and what will not.

The old style 'vanity publishers' had a very bad reputation – they took your book with all its errors, and charged a huge amount of money to produce a limited number of books. You were (most unfairly in my opinion) at the mercy of ridicule. These days it's a fully accepted part of the industry and open to everyone. In fact, some mainstream publishing houses are very keen to consider authors who have been through the process, and have a proven record in making sales within the industry.

Employing A Self-Publishing Service Provider

This is where the author chooses a reputable self-publishing firm to work with – hereafter called a *service provider* – and funds the whole operation themselves. There are many such firms, large and small, and these can be found on the Internet, through advertisements in the many writers' magazines, or by recommendation. Their websites will outline what's on offer, from a basic package to a more expensive personal service, but if you're unsure of what you want, or feel a bit intimidated with figures and provisions, any worthy firm will be happy to talk to you on the phone, or by email. When one is on the nursery slopes, personal contact is very re-assuring so be very wary of any firm that does everything online, is impossible to get through to on the phone, or who doesn't reply quickly to an email.

In choosing a firm you'll most likely be offered variations on an easily understood publishing package deal. The lowest cost will be for the basic paperback production, using your perfected computer manuscript, and being provided with a cover from a standard range to choose from. If you want your work brought out in hardback then this will be a bespoke negotiated price. Thereafter, the cost goes up for any 'add-ons' you feel you may need. Add-ons include editing, the creation of a bespoke cover, and various levels of marketing and publicity, with most firms happy to create a tailor-made deal for you. In addition, your service provider should put your book up for sale on Amazon, and the many other online purchasing opportunities, all detailed later in the sales section.

There will also be varying deals offered as to how you're 'paid' for sales, and most firms will offer a 'royalty' payment on each book they sell for you. As every book is different, i.e. the size, word count, and retail price, your service provider will work out your rate when these have been agreed. A ballpark figure would be around 55% of *net* price – again to be agreed in detail. Whatever you get, it'll be much, much more than you'd get from a mainstream deal, but ensure you're told in advance when your royalty payment dates and statements are due. Another advantage is that they will be pleased to supply you with books to sell yourself at a very heavily discounted price – something around half of the agreed sale price. However, you won't get a royalty payment on books you sell yourself, as these aren't factored into your recorded sales figures.

In going ahead with a service provider I recommend that you take your time to work out all the financial implications, using *what you can afford to lose* as a yardstick. Remember that you love your work and you're sure it'll sell well, but sales in any form of publishing are not guaranteed. If you *do* sell well the deal can be excellent, but if you don't you might find yourself out of pocket.

Once you're satisfied, and have agreed to a deal, you'll be expected to sign a contract. Although this is usually a simple agreement between yourself and the service provider, do read it thoroughly to ensure you fully understand all the clauses as you'll be taking full responsibility for the content. Most contracts, in every part of the industry, are so standardised that things rarely go wrong, but still check your work will be registered under copyright law with the UK Copyright Office. Here it will be officially recognised as yours in a court of law, and if any texts are reproduced (plagiarised) without your permission, it's a prosecuting offence. It's very rare with self-publishing that your *publishing rights* are signed over, but make sure that this is not the case. If the agreement needs be terminated for any reason – one reason could be that you've been offered a mainstream contract – you'll want to take the whole package with you.

Having happily signed the contract, and paid your fee, there should be no other outlay unless you decide to upgrade any provision at a later date. You will send off your final completed manuscript by email attachment, and your firm will take over the production. They will set it up into standard printed book form, and provide you with an ISBN (an International Standard Book Number) and a bar code. There will be much more on ISBN numbers later, but every book that goes through the tills, or is sold online as an eBook, has to have this identifying number as a legal requirement. Once all the groundwork is done, and your book is in an 'oven ready' form, it'll be sent for printing to a 'Print-on-Demand' firm; the biggest firm of which in the UK is the very excellent Lightning Source, UK. On receipt it'll be stored electronically so orders can be processed in any amounts, from one single copy to multiples requested. Distribution of your book within the trade is a large area covered later in The Book Industry section, but initially check with your service provider how many books you're obliged to order *en bloc*, and what arrangements are made for distribution through wholesalers.

After reading this section you might feel that there's an awful lot to do to self-publish, and being in charge of the whole operation can put the fear of God into one, but remember that a reputable service provider will hold your hand every step of the way. Their reputation, in an intensely competitive market, is very important to them, so each one should be offering a smooth, professional, and transparent journey to the production of the completed book.

The Book Cover: A Huge Consideration

Although mainstream publishers can occasionally get it wrong, one of the key areas where self-published books are often found wanting is the cover. The primary comments, especially from bookshop owners, are that they're often dull, cheap looking, unimaginative, and poorly executed. *All* book covers need to be eye-catching, professional, and appropriate to the content, and it's another very difficult area to get right. I'd suggest that you take the time to go into bookshops and look at some of the covers on display. Really look at the front cover, the back cover, and the spine. Take a step back and stare. Which books are leaping out to you and saying 'buy me'? Which ones disappear into the background as being dull and dreary? What type of designs and colours attract you, and are appropriate to your book? Obviously, the cover of a lively romantic comedy will have a vastly different appeal to that of a dark thriller, or historical work, so identify your market.

As part of a standard package your service provider will offer you some fairly basic cover images that can be re-produced without much tinkering, or (if you pay for a bespoke cover) will provide you with the services of their in-house art designer. If you're still not happy you can provide your own image, and for a tsunami of choice look up some of the online photo library firms such as Istock (www.istockphoto.com), Alamy (www.alamy.com), Fotosearch (www.fotosearch.com), and Bigstock (www.bigstock.com). Some charge a large fee for an image or design, some very little, but always ensure their terms of trading state that the one you want is 'royalty free'.

Some of them, such as Bigstock, are very reasonable and use a system of 'credits', currently £30 for ten credits. To purchase your chosen image you release X number of credits, according to the size of pixels required. However, they insist that you must pay for each differing *marketing usage*, i.e. 1) the cover, 2) the publicity materials and 3) email material. Once you've paid for an image of your choice you can then work with your service provider's design department until they come up with something you're happy with.

Initially, it's the cover that sells your book, so be prepared to be fussy, even if you end up paying a bit extra for a bespoke design. It's a huge folly to cut corners. You don't go to an interview in scruffy jeans and a T-shirt, do you? Present your book as a well turned out candidate; suited, booted, with attractive accessories and no skimping on quality.

The Back Cover
The back cover blurb is an enormous opportunity, together

with your intriguing and enticing opening chapter, to secure a sale. Spend some quality time examining a great many books, and decide what works well in *commercial* terms. It'll need a clever paragraph to draw the buyer in, similar to the example I included on *Jane Eyre* in the Literary Agent Submissions section. It should be informative and enticing and give a real flavour of what's to come. Maybe write two or three practice pieces and ask for the opinion of anyone who has *not* read your book, or knows much about it, so you get 'a buyers eye'.

Cover Endorsements

Another idea, for inclusion on both the front and back cover, is to try and get a pre-publication endorsement. We've all seen book covers emblazoned with a line of glowing praise, sometimes from a well-known personality or best-selling author. Here are some examples

'*An exciting tale of drama on the high seas, written with energy and enthusiasm. A great read.*' Jack Jones

'*A captivating, emotional story of a wartime love affair. A real page-turner. The characters will remain with me for a very long time*'. Jackie Jones

'*The very best book on bread making I have ever read*'. Paul Hollywood (only joking!)

But how do you get one? Mainstream publishers often get someone to oblige through their own contacts, and many use other authors on their client lists in a mutual backslapping exercise. But if you're self-published then it'll be far harder, unless you're well connected. If you *do* know someone (or even if a friend of a friend knows someone) then it's worth asking. The daughter-in-law of one author I know worked with the son of a famous actress. Contact was made and the actress came up trumps!

Even if they have no connection at all with the book's content a 'name' on the cover will always be a huge bonus. When approaching anyone, famous or not, don't be pushy, or 'big up' your book, and always give a realistic timescale for a response.

The real problem the self-published find is that the book cover has to be finalised before the book itself is produced. The endorsement on the cover of my last novel's paperback version was obtained from a very pro-active readers group in my nearest large library, long before I'd found a publisher. I printed out four extremely heavy A4 paper copies and the group heroically carried them home to read. It's not ideal, but emailed copies could be used much more effectively, with the growth of reading devices. By the time the eBook version came out I was able to glean my best review for inclusion.

Alert: be prepared to be let down! Busy people lead busy lives and with the best will in the world they might not like what they've read, or forget about it altogether. If this happens you have to bite this particular bullet, but if you're fortunate enough to get the nod from a well-known 'name', exploit it ruthlessly.

An extra word of advice. Your frontispiece will always make it obvious who your publisher is, so its status as 'self-published' has to be overcome. I've always stated, absolutely truthfully, that self-publishing is becoming a very accepted method of publication, and with slimmed down publishing houses rarely taking a risk on a newcomer, many authors of quality now self-publish and do very well for themselves. However, an element of discrimination *can* exist in some sections of the book world (dare I mention mainstream authors still luxuriating within their contracts?) and there will always be some who'll dismiss your book out of hand. My advice is to believe in yourself and your work, develop a thick skin, and get over it. You have invested a large part of your life in your book, you love it, you know it's good, and you must be loyal to it, so don't be at all diffident.

Self-Publishing Success

I'd now like to introduce you to a very successful children's author, John Kitchen (wjkitchen@gmail.com), who has written about his publishing experiences. His first novel *Nicola's Ghost* was self-published, and won first prize in the Writers' Digest Award as Best Young Adult Novel of 2011. This led to his second and third, published mainstream; *A Spectre in the Stones* (Thames River Press 2013) and *Jax' House* (Union Bridge Press, 2015). In addition he has self-published a delightful illustrated book for much younger children, *Kamazu's Big Swing Band*.

My Experiences in Self-Publishing, by John Kitchen

My experience of self-publishing led me to *New Generation Publishing,* having already gone through various important hoops. My manuscript, *Nicola's Ghost,* had been critiqued by a literary consultancy– in my case *The Oxford Literary Consultancy* – and, with their support, I was taken on by a literary agent. However, our attempts at getting the book published were unsuccessful, possibly because I had no established readership and was totally unknown as a writer, making publishing my book too risky. In discussion, my agent and I felt that it might be a good step to self-publish *Nicola's Ghost* because, in that way, I would have the opportunity to build up a readership and make a traditional deal for a second book more likely.

We first self-published with a large company who produced a very impressive edition. However *Nicola's Ghost* is written for young people and the publisher set the retail price at £11.99, well out of reach for most children. So we moved to *New Generation Publishing.*

It was an excellent decision. Their director, Daniel Cooke, worked very closely with me in producing the book, consulting me fully, discussing size, type, information to go on the cover, and agreeing to use the same cover design as was used in the original version. The result, published in exactly the same dimensions as the original, retailed at £6.99 – a much more realistic price.

The advantage of using a company like *New Generation* is that they do everything; registering your book, establishing copyright, creating the ISBN number and controlling distribution through all the major outlets. You don't have to find space at home to store hundreds of copies, or be bothered with distribution. All that is done for you. They provide sales outlets for your book, by uploading it on Amazon, listing it with all book suppliers who sell through major bookshops, and getting it into marketing catalogues. They also ensure the royalties flow in at regular intervals, together with a breakdown of where and how your book has been sold. The royalties are considerably higher than they would be for a traditional deal and in *New Generation's* case they offer you support and advice whenever you need it.

I worked tirelessly promoting the book (and myself) although self-promotion does not come easily to me (I am, believe it or not, a very retiring guy!). I persuaded my local press to cover my visits to schools and they also kindly agreed to do a feature on me. I contacted my local radio station and was interviewed on a chat show. I prepared publicity leaflets using *Vista Print* and circulated these to schools and, as a result, I was invited into over thirty schools to do 'Writers' Workshops' and to sell signed copies of *Nicola's Ghost.* I also did talks to local adult groups and libraries. *New Generation* downloaded an eBook version on Amazon, featured it on its website home page, listed it as a 'recommended read', and linked my own website to theirs, which considerably raised my own profile.

Daniel Cooke, of *New Generation Publishing* has a blog and issues news bulletins on their website. He mentioned *Nicola's Ghost* and its various successes on several occasion as a means of promoting the book. If anything big happens he also produces and circulates Press releases. I believe he works on the principle that, if a writer is pro-active in marketing and selling his book, then he will offer support and help in any way he can.

I also benefited from a special deal that *New Generation* have with their authors. Each year a small number of good quality and successful books are awarded *The New Generation Publishing Award* which means the traditional mainstream arm of the company, *Legend Press,* takes over and markets the book as they would a mainstream publication. *Nicola's Ghost* was fortunate enough to win this award and was subsequently submitted for a competition in the US, run by *The Writers' Digest.* It won first prize in the Young Adult category as: 'Best Self-Published Young Adult Novel 2011'.

So far, I have sold over a thousand copies of *Nicola's Ghost.* If I had not self-published I would not have built up an enthusiastic and growing readership, and wouldn't have won two prestigious prizes. These prizes were very definitely a career boost as in 2013, through my agent, I was offered a mainstream publishing deal with Thames River Press. My first book with them, *The Spectre in the Stones* has already sold several hundred copies, and my second, *Jax' House*, will be published (by the newly created imprint Union Bridge Press) in 2015.

To conclude. Self-publishing is really worth it and I have found *New Generation Publishing* remarkably supportive. Daniel Cooke, on hearing that I had secured a traditional deal for *A Spectre in the Stones*, phoned my agent to ask if he should issue a press release about my success! Now... did you have any idea that self-publishing concerns would go that far in support of their authors? The self-publishing scene is certainly changing, and that is really good news for all prospective authors. (www.johnkitchenauthor.com)

Creating an Online 'Do-it-Yourself' Production

Online services, such as *Lulu*, and Amazon's *CreateSpace*, are another option. This means you set up and produce the book yourself by following an explanatory template in the hope that it'll measure up to a professionally produced book. I'm told that 'it's easy' and those with basic understanding of computer technology will be competent, but it's certainly not for technophobes. The services are free – yes – absolutely free, *but* you'll have no personal contact if something goes wrong. Amazon seem to be taking over this type of publishing in a serious way, with genre imprints, such as Thomas and Mercer, and I understand they're even offering successful authors publishing 'contracts'. Thus, we can expect this area to develop even more in the future.

Using a 'Print Only' Firm

Some firms, such as Anthoney Rowe and CMP(UK)Ltd, offer a litho option, and this method of production, due to the quality of the paper and print, is far superior to the usual paperback. This might be of interest to non-fiction writers with a waiting market. The deal is that you send them your completed manuscript, and then liaise closely with them on the production. You will decide how many copies (called units) you wish to be produced 'in bulk', and the more you order the lower the unit price drops. Thus, an order of 300 will cost you much more 'per unit', than an order of 3000. If you're confident you have a waiting market for your book – such as an educational textbook or a one-off quality production – you'll make much more profit on sales if you order the larger amount. But it's still a huge gamble that you'll sell your stock. I understand that they now offer a POD service, and this is welcome news, but you will have to get your book formatted to publishing standard as they don't offer any services other than producing your book.

Crowd Funding

It's only very recently that I've discovered something called *Crowd Funding*. You may have heard of this method of raising funds in all walks of life, and this has moved to the book industry. A number of what one would call 'famous names' are doing this, so I have to conclude that Crowd Funding must be taken seriously.

Author Alice Jolly (www. alicejolly.com) has chosen to go down this route, and as it's something very new to me I interviewed Alice in an attempt to find out alot more. Alice is using *Unbound* (http://unbound.co.uk) to produce her sensitive memoir, *Dead Babies and Seaside Towns*, based on her personal life experiences, and this was successfully funded and published in summer, 2015. She had previously published two novels with Simon and Schuster, had four plays produced by the Everyman Theatre in Cheltenham, and teaches creative writing on the MSt at Oxford University.

Using Crowd Funding – An Interview with Alice Jolly

Mary: Crowd Funding is only something I've vaguely heard about and have never taken much interest in. Through one of your articles on www.Authorselectric I discovered the Crowd Funding firm, *Unbound*, which uses this method to publish a wide range of books, some by very well known names. As you've used this method to bring out your current book can you explain why you chose to use crowd funding.

Alice: I decided to try the crowd funding approach for *Dead Babies and Seaside Towns* because I hadn't had a good experience with traditional publishing. My first novel had been publicised and distributed well, but my second book received no attention at all. I liked the idea of crowd funding because I think that we desperately need to find new ways of publishing books. I teach Creative Writing and I see so much good work being rejected. The traditional publishing industry doesn't work well for books that don't fit into a specific genre or format, so I was happy to work with people who are trying to do something new.

Mary: If you find you need much more explanation as to what's involved are you able to talk to someone at the firm directly, on a one-to-one basis?

Alice: Absolutely. When *Unbound* first agreed to publish my book, I spent a couple of hours talking it over with them. They then made the film about the book, and since that time I have been in touch with them constantly. They always got back to me very quickly. They also sent out updates letting me know how many people had subscribed. They have also helped to publicise the book.

Mary: You obviously thought it was a realistic possibility. How much money did you have to try and raise?

Alice: I had to raise just over £12,000. I started in November 2014 and by March 2015, five months later, I was 90% of the way there.

Mary: How did you start your campaign to raise pledges?

Alice: First I e-mailed everyone I know. I then started using Facebook and Twitter which I'd never done before. I've written blog posts, articles, and book reviews and I've also tapped into networks of people who have been through the same kind of experiences as I have.

Mary: If one wishes to pledge a fixed sum, how is this done?

Alice: If you look on the website you can see how to choose the amount you want to pledge. It could be £10, £20, £50, £100, £500. From then on you just follow the instructions in the same way as you would when making any online purchase.

Mary: Are all pledge payments receipted?

Alice: Yes, everyone who pledges gets a receipt. They probably also receive a questionnaire about why they signed up. Unbound are very keen to have that information. Also, everyone who has signed up has access to my 'Writers' Shed'. That means they get updates from me about how the process is going. People like that. They like to feel part of the production process of the book.

Mary: Did you find it involved a great deal of work?

Alice: It has been a lot of work and it has certainly pushed me to do things that I don't normally do. However, the truth is that no matter how you publish your book, you are going to have to spend quite a bit of time on publicity. The difference with *Unbound* is that you do a lot before the book is published. But that means you can do less afterwards. Also it won't be so hard if I do it a second time. I now have contact with all the people who have subscribed, I have a good e-mail list, and I've raised my profile on social media. All this is what you have to do, anyway.

Mary: What happens if you don't get enough pledges and you have to pull out? Do the investors get their money back?

Alice: Yes. If a book doesn't go ahead then investors do get their money back. I'm not aware that, so far, any *Unbound* books haven't gone ahead. I think sometimes it takes people a long time to raise the money – and they have to be very creative to do it – but most people will get there in the end.

Thank you very much, Alice, for agreeing to be interviewed. *Dead Babies and Seaside Towns* is now available for sale on Amazon, in all formats.

Chapter 5 : My Own Publishing Experiences

Mainstream

My first novel, *The Crowded Bed*, was published in 2007 by Transita, a mainstream publisher. The cover was lovely, I was paid a very nice advance, and pre-publication publicity was sent out to bookshops and libraries via trade catalogues and online retail sales sites. I was visited at home by their marketing and publicity manager, the local media was contacted, and Transita's sales reps gave it their best pitch to bookshops. However, despite all strenuous efforts, I was a first time author, with no fanfare or hype, and it was still an uphill task to get my book noticed. With no further budget to invest, it became down to me to try and make sales. But at least I had a very firm base to build upon and there's no better way to get stuck in than . . . to get stuck in!

As this was eight years ago there were no online media platforms to join, and the only methods open were what I will call 'the personal way'. I arranged face-to-face meetings with bookshop owners, sent printed publicity material to libraries, offered to do talks to reading groups, set up a local radio interview, and devised various other innovative methods, of which there will be much more later in the marketing and publicity sections. It was very hard work, but my efforts paid off and I was lucky to sell most of my print run of 2,500. Transita then broke the bad news that they had decided not to publish any more fiction. My two-book deal collapsed and (devastated) I was left without a publisher.

Self-Publishing with Litho Printing

Nothing daunted! Boosted by my sales figures, and huge confidence, I self-published my second novel in 2008, using a litho print run of 2,000 at around £2.00 a book. I chose the cover myself from a stock photo library (at around £100.00), and my print provider, although saying it wasn't a very good image, agreed to use it. It was a mistake. The production showed that the pixels were insufficient, and the result was an amateur looking blur. But I was stuck with it. Despite all my best efforts, I only managed to sell 800 of my stock, and the residue had to be pulped. I'm not saying 'don't do' litho printing, as it's obvious you have the potential to make money, especially if you have a guaranteed sales base. I *did* end up in profit, but only after they had taken statutory expenses and monthly stock storage charges.

Self-Publishing With a Service Provider

I am a member of *The Oxford Writers' Group*, a longstanding group of writers who have become firm friends. The group consists of mainly fiction writers (for both the adult and children's markets), two successful journalists, and a poet. In 2005 we formed a publishing consortium, *OxPens*. The idea was to produce a slim volume of short stories, all based in Oxford. Thirteen of us (about three-quarters of the membership) contributed to a publishing fund, and one of our non-contributing members acted as editor (an heroic labour of love). We spent a great deal of time on the cover, wanting to display a feeling of academic Oxford, and were very lucky in being able to use a stunning watercolour impression of the traditional Oxford skyline, painted by the renowned Oxford watercolour artist Valerie Petts. The final manuscript was dispatched to our chosen service provider, and thereafter all the technical production work was undertaken for us. It was printed by Lightning Source, and the result was *The Sixpenny Debt and Other Oxford Stories*.

We genuinely had no aspirations for commercial success; the concept was merely born out of the idea to have a 'memoir' of ourselves, and just hoped we would sell enough copies to cover our initial expenses. Having no one but ourselves as the publicity and marketing force, we all pitched in with sales ideas. We paid up-front for 200 copies, one of the members generously offered to store the bulk order, and we started a concerted campaign in Oxford city. We visited every retailer we thought might be prepared to sell it, including bookshops and tourist outlets, and left a 'for approval' copy with them. The offer was for them to order directly from us, and within a few weeks the book was stocked all over the city, including Blackwells and Waterstones. It sold very well in both shops, and Waterstones even talked it up as a 'recommended read' by placing it next to the till and dedicating it an in-store shelf. Within a couple of months it had been taken up by The Oxfordshire County Library Service and many small independent bookshops in the county.

In the summer of 2008 we produced a second volume, *The Lost College and Other Oxford Stories*. Colin Dexter, the creator of the renowned Inspector Morse series, very generously gave us both a front cover quote and a foreword, and Waterstones gave us a quote for the back cover (referring to *The Sixpenny Debt*):

'We couldn't possibly have imagined its immense popularity – it became the biggest non-discounted seller in the whole shop in 2007. And what a book!'
Waterstones

The Lost College was just as successful. A third volume, *The Bodleian Murders* was published in 2010, and a fourth *The Midnight Press* was released in 2013. A fifth is in planning. This is a case of what you can do to find a market for a book with a strong local bias. To date our anthologies have sold over 3000 copies, and we can boast twelve other OxPens publications by our members.

A Return to Mainstream

In 2012 I signed a two-book deal with Thames River Press. *The Priest, His Lady and The Drowned Child* (a re-print of my 2008 self-published novel, *A Man Like Any Other*) was published in 2013, and my third novel, *Who Was Angela Zendalic?* in 2014.

And Back Again!

Calling All Authors is self-published by *New Generation Publishing*

Part Four:

Publishing an eBook

Chapter 6 : It's Big Business!

Soaring Sales

eBook production is a huge business and figures are suggesting that eBook sales are overtaking those of printed books. Many eBook authors are selling huge amounts, with sales figures that vastly trump those of paperback 'bestsellers'. However, having very little media coverage, it's likely they're only famous amongst their fan bases and the eBook community. If you're considering this route, then you will, of course, be in competition with thousands of other hopefuls, so the more you can find out about the eBook industry, the better.

Manuscript Preparation

Preparing your manuscript for the eBook market requires the same amount of meticulous attention to detail required for any form of paper print publication (covered previously in Quality Control). It will not be the responsibility of your eBook producer to correct your text (even though they might be prepared to tidy it up a little) so your work will be published 'as is'. It'll be read on an eBook reader device screen, in exactly the same way as a paperback page, so make sure that all previous editing advice is followed.

Technology and Formatting

Although the market leader in eBook display is Amazon Kindle, there are also many others, such as Kobo, Nook, and Apple. If you have extensive technical computer knowledge, you *can* put an eBook up online yourself, but the formatting is a much trickier skill than that of a d-i-y paperback, and needs to be perfect. Therefore, if you don't have the technological skills (and that includes most of us) you should employ an expert in the field. Basically, margins have to line up, paragraphs need indentation, section breaks need spacing, and new chapter headings need to be placed at the top of new pages. I've often read an eBook on my Kindle where the set-up has been very wonky in places (I expect you have as well), so a professional production is essential. The cost is not prohibitive, and it's a very good deal indeed.

KDP (Kindle Direct Publishing)

If you choose to set up your book with KDP, the market leader in eBook publishing, your title will be put on Amazon for a standard price, and the Kindle Owner's Lending Library. You have a choice of choosing 70% royalty or 35%. If you choose the lower royalty your book will be included in Kindle Unlimited which offers the author further marketing options and sale incentives. I'm not able to reproduce the whole of their author information here, as I found it was quite complicated, but you can read all relevant information on their website, or have an in-depth talk with your eBook service provider. Many eBook producers are to be found online, and there are many differing opportunities on offer, but the only option you have is to work your way through them, and decide which will be the best deal for you.

In order to get a real feel for eBook publishing I've interviewed Andy Severn, CEO of Oxford eBooks Ltd; a leader in the field of eBook production.

All About eBook Production – An Interview with Andy Severn (www.oxford-ebooks.com)

Mary: Thank you for agreeing to be interviewed, Andy, as I know you're always incredibly busy, producing hundreds of eBooks per year. eBooks are certainly the fastest growing trend in publishing, both for fiction and non-fiction, so can I start by asking you how you came to start up the business.

Andy: I had tinkered with sci-fi-writing for many years and self-published them as eBooks. In those days, eBooks were very basic and distribution channels were few and far between. My background is about twenty-five years in the computer games industry, and was fortunate enough to work for a games developer that also had a science fiction publishing arm. I became involved with the eBooks production there, applied my own scant knowledge to the operation, and set up the distribution and production pipeline there. In 2010 I left the company due to redundancy and decided I would try to make a living on what I had learned.

Mary: Due to many factors, the world of publishing has certainly changed in the last five years. It's very difficult to get a mainstream contract, and thus the growth in self-publishing and the eBook has been phenomenal. What type of authors are contacting you for information?

Andy: I hear from all kinds of people and it's interesting to see the wide variety of books that people want to self-publish. There are quite a few people with their personal memoirs and topics that I suppose mainstream publishers would struggle to make a profit on. Self-publishing is a wonderful platform to give voice to the kinds of content that would normally not be possible to access.

Mary: One of the main attractions of publishing an eBook is the relatively low cost in setting up the operation, and the attractive 'royalties' paid out on sales. Can you explain a little more about the economic factors involved?

Andy: One of the biggest marketplaces for eBooks is Amazon. I find that it's particularly attractive as it's relatively simple to set up an account and upload eBooks. In most cases, Amazon will pay up to 70% of the list price of the eBook in royalties, which is higher than the e-industry standard of around 50% from other distributors.

eBook production costs are fairly low – say, £150, and maybe another £100 if you want to have a cover artwork produced. It's easy to see that if you pitch your eBook at just a couple of pounds, you'd only need to sell a couple of hundred copies to start making money. Self-publishing as an eBook is certainly a low risk method to get your masterpiece in the marketplace.

Another aspect of self-publishing that should not be ignored is the print edition. This is now very affordable with the rise of Print on Demand (POD). Although certainly a lower margin is offered, due to the necessity to physically print and distribute the books, and the large slice the booksellers take (40-50%). However, it's always nice to be able to hold a printed copy of your masterpiece, or see it for sale in a shop. We've thus diversified into POD as well, and find that we're getting a lot more business in that area now.

Mary: Once a client has agreed to go ahead with you, what comes next? I presume they send you off their 'finished' work and leave you to do all the technical transcribing. As with all self-publishing, is it up to the client to ensure the quality of the manuscript, or do you advise on editing?

Andy: Yes, all I need is the manuscript and production can start. It's important that the manuscript *is* finished and complete, though if any glaring errors are found we'll fix them on the fly and let the author know what we found. The beauty of digital text is that changes *are* easy to make and generally we're happy to fix up the occasional author's typo after the event without charge.

Mary: If the client is sufficiently concerned that their work might not be up to scratch do you offer an editing service?

Andy: Yes. Oxford eBooks also publishes selected works, so has the capacity to offer proofreading and editing if needed.

Mary: Once you take on the work, what technical transcribing processes do you put it through?

Andy: We have our own eBook production software that has been written specifically to take all the hard work out of transcribing the original manuscript into a raw form that can be used to produce an eBook. Generally, this involves a number of 'cleaning' passes that standardises the text, font, removes unnecessary spaces, formatting etc. Once we have a clean text file, we apply final formatting to make it look good on an eBook reader, as well as any book-specific design that the author wants. If the manuscript is without any particular style, we'll apply a clean house-style or suggest a little formatting to fancy it up a little.

The final process, again using bespoke software in conjunction with industry-standard format verification tools, turns the intermediate formatted text into the final eBook files, coded for all types of eBook reader. The files are then tested on a number of simulators, as well as actual reader devices, to make sure that any formatting and design looks perfect. Generally, eBooks are checked on iPad, Kindle, iPhone, Nook, Android, as well as PC / Mac readers such as Adobe Digital Editions.

Mary: Although the eBook doesn't have a conventional cover it'll need a mock cover plate to display on Amazon Kindle's lists. Do you offer an art service if the client isn't confident enough to produce their own?

Andy: Yes, we have a couple of really talented artists working with us that are able to produce illustrations for the internals as well as fully painted covers. That costs a little more so the author on a budget, with maybe just £100 to spend, can opt for a much less expensive option involving compositing and manipulation of high quality stock photography.

Mary: Once the work is 'good to go' what are the processes involved in putting it up on Amazon?

Andy: Amazon make the process very simple. It's possible to complete the entire process in just a couple of minutes. Okay, I've done it hundreds of times and I'm used to it, but there's nothing particularly technical there. There are a few tricks though. There's an option to add key words – choose these well, as they'll help your book to be discovered. Also, you can put your book in up to two categories. Choose one that's pretty mainstream, but then make your second one relatively genre specific. Amazon have about five million books on the catalogue and if your book starts to sell a handful of copies a day then chances are that you'll then appear in the top 100 for the obscure genre. That'll show up on the sales page on Amazon and presto, your book is in the charts! That will impress potential readers.

Setting the price of your book is pretty simple too. They'll calculate the prevailing rates for the various countries they sell in, so try to think in terms of the price in U.S. dollars. Then let them work the rest out for you. A new thing that Amazon have is a calculator that will suggest the best price for your book based on its genre – I've tried it and managed to get a noticeable increase in revenue from some titles. They will also work out the 'new' rates of Vat that have recently been imposed on eProductions by the EEC.

Mary: Thereafter, the eBook is available for customer download. Can you explain the royalties the authors can expect, and how they're paid?

Andy: Amazon now pay your royalties directly into your bank account! They pay monthly, and you'll get a payment from each of their dozen or so main territories in which you've made sales. They'll also pay you in sterling, so you don't need a U.S. bank account any more. Royalties are paid 3 months in arrears, so you'll need to wait a little while after publishing for the money to come rolling in. It's also worth filling in the new online form on the Amazon dashboard that allows you to avoid the 30% tax withholding that the U.S government take from U.S based royalties.

Mary: Most authors will be trying to make sales, and it's a very difficult area to advise on. Do you have a basic sales and marketing advice sheet?

Andy: Further to choosing your key words and categories carefully, make sure your description is well written. Take your time over this and make it something that's going to draw the reader in and make them buy it. Readers can download the first few pages of your eBook for free, so make sure your opening pages are fantastic. Reviews are also another one of the best ways to attract more sales. Try to encourage genuine readers to post reviews of your book – though beware! They take a dim view of people posting their own. Local newspapers are a good source of publicity, so see if they're interested in reviewing your book, or doing a local interest story.

Mary: My own thoughts are that it's the genre writers, i.e. romance, crime, fantasy, espionage, and sci-fi who are most likely to have a specific reader source, due to a network of keen readers. Do you think this is true?

Andy: It's certainly true that the genres will be able to sell books simply off the back of the established reader base. However, there are always exceptions to this, or emerging genres that can be tapped. One eBook I published late in 2012, *Shackled To My Family*, was written by an author who had suffered a terrible existence at the hands of her overbearing and abusive Muslim family. This book was a great success as it had a very particular appeal to a number of women (and, as I discovered, men) who had been in similar situations of forced marriage and abuse. The author, Samina Younis was featured in newspapers, and appeared on radio (both local and national) and TV to talk about her ordeals. As a result eBook sales have been brisk, and we have now come full circle in the publishing world and are offering this book in paperback form. As I said earlier, self-publishing is probably helping otherwise hidden gems to emerge.

Mary: Have you any idea why some authors make incredible sales of thousands and some don't.

Andy: There are many reasons – I suspect that much of the time, an author will run out of steam at the marketing stage. Writers just like to write and they're rarely salespeople. That's where the traditional publishing route has its advantages, as there should be a team of crack marketing staff to make sure the book sells. But then publishers probably only publish a tiny fraction of the manuscripts they receive and even then it takes years to go to press.

Mary: There have been many examples of successful eBook authors being taken up by mainstream publishing houses. Is this a sign of the times that publishers take eBook sales very seriously.

Andy: Publishers certainly take eBooks seriously as their sales figures have overtaken those of the printed book. The costs of production are a fraction of the print process, and so their margins are better. Consider; if a self-publisher can afford to put a book up on sale themselves it's nothing for a large publisher to do the same.

Mary: Finally. Thank you so much for all the immensely useful information you have given readers of this book. My last question is; how do you see the future and do you ever see eBooks overtaking paperbacks?

Andy: As said, sales have already reportedly overtaken printed books on Amazon. However, I don't see the demise of the paper book in the foreseeable future. eBooks have the great advantage of being immediately available. You can buy one in minutes at any time day or night, read it anywhere – especially if you're one of those people who read on their Smartphone. There is an increasing number of people who will probably now only rarely buy a book in printed form, preferring to just buy one (often for less) to read on their iPhone. But, encouragingly for fiction in general, these people are now more inclined to read because there's less *effort* involved, and what's more, people are reading more than ever before. That's *got* to be good news for authors everywhere.

Successful eBook Authors

Marketing and publicising an eBook is significantly different to paper printed versions. There doesn't seem to be any recipe for sure-fire success, as what works well for one doesn't work for another. All I can pick up is that it needs a concentrated effort, and a great deal of hard work, to fight your way through the jungle of methods available. However, judging by the amount of authors I meet who have done well, results can be excellent. It will become apparent that successful eBook authors are successful in different ways, and here you can read the experiences of four of them.

Debrah Martin writes in three genres; literary fiction, thriller fiction (as D.B.Martin), and YA fiction (as Lily Stuart). She also teaches and mentors in creative writing and independent publishing. The following article is an excerpt from her own marketing and publicity material, and is reproduced with her kind permission. More information about her books, workshops and mentoring can be found on her website: www.debrahmartin.co.uk

How I Sell My Books on The Internet: Debrah Martin

How do I sell my books on the internet? I'm radical. No – not politically, or even behaviourally (unless it's after a glass or two). It's a mnemonic for how I approach selling my books, and is based on:

Readability
Accessibility
Discoverability
Interesting the right audience
Credibility
Adding value
Letting it flow…

All are important but I'm going to concentrate on just two here: **discoverability** and **interesting the right audience**; two absolute essentials for you to be 'found' as an author.

Discoverability:
So your book and 12 million others are swilling around on Amazon. You check your KDP dashboard and find you have no sales – not even a sniff of one, in fact; why? You need to be 'found', and there are a number of things you need to do to achieve this. Amazon, Smashwords, Lulu and all of the sales platforms are really just giant search engines. You look online, type in the sort of thing you're looking for and the site offers you a selection of things matching your preferences; thousands of them . . . If it's a potato peeler, there'll be all manner and make of them. If it's a book there are all kinds of categories and genres, so you need to establish the words, phrases and lists readers might look in to find a book like yours; in other words, keywords and categories.

- **Categories** – are the genres your book falls into. For example, on the left hand side of the Amazon page there are lists of eBook categories –thrillers, literary, romance etc. Click on one of them – say mystery – and you'll find more options. As of today I found these possible mystery categories:

  Women Sleuths (14,751)
  Police Procedurals (8,654)

Hard-Boiled (6,979)
Private Investigators (5,594)
Collections & Anthologies (4,793)
Cozy (6,446)
Mystery (10,185)
Historical (6,779)
International Mystery & Crime (3,731)
Cozy Animal Mystery

The numbers after the description are the number of books currently on sale in that sub-category of mystery. Drill down further and you'll find yet more sub-categories. Your mission is to find the subcategory that best fits your book, but with the least competition in it. That way, when a potential reader looks in the category, hey presto! They find your book high up on the list. Discoverability!

Why are categories so important? It's all to do with achieving the highest ranking you can in that category because when a potential reader searches for a book, you want to be one of the first books they find.

• **Keywords** are the words people use to further define what they're looking for within a category. They need to relate specifically to your book as well. They're trickier than finding the right category because there are infinite possibilities. How do you decide? There are two answers to this, the long one and the short one:

The long answer requires you to research what other books similar to yours have used for keywords. You can do this by typing in various suitable words and phrases in the search bar on Amazon and reviewing the results. It's a time consuming process, but done logically and patiently, will produce some solid keywords. You are ultimately looking for keywords that are popularly searched for, but do not simply pitch you up against major competition.

The short answer is make use of some of the software that is available which can draw off popular keyword phrases based on a sample you input, suggest other suitable variations and provide you with the statistics relevant to each keyword – popularity of use, average rankings of other books using the same keyword, average pricing and the average number of reviews those books have. From these statistics, you can determine the most helpful keywords and phrases to apply to your book to be able to compete. I use two pieces of software that can do this and cover them in full in my workshops and mentoring work (see my website www.debrahmartin.co.uk for more details).

- Also make sure you have an author platform – your shop window, if you like. It should include a website, a social media presence and an Author's page on both Amazon.com and Amazon.co.uk if you are selling your books through Amazon (generally a good idea given Amazon's reach).

Interesting the right audience:
Do you have a mailing list so you can tell your avid readers when your next book is going to be released? Or when a book is on offer? If you haven't you should.

Of course it's wonderful to see the graph of sales on your KDP dashboard rising, but not all of those purchasers will become readers, and if they do, not all of those readers will remember to look out for your next release. But your mailing list members will, because you will remind them . . .

So how do you generate a mailing list? By having an incentive for someone to sign up to it. Incentives can come in all forms – free books, sample chapters, novellas, or prizes. You can provide them through competitions and giveaways, such as via Twitter and sites that will specifically organise and run a competition or giveaway for you. You can promote it in one of your books, or you can use social media and an incentive to encourage sign-ups. You can even run a competition through Amazon itself or reader's sites such as Goodreads. And a mailing list will not just enable you to promote your books directly to its members. It paves the way to:

> Gaining reviews.
> Gaining more exposure.
> Promoting special offers.
> Helping launch new releases.
> Helping achieve best seller status.

Get yourself to the internet and get a mailing list, now!

Using a combination of these and other strategies, my books have hit #1 bestsellers in their categories several times each. Yours can too . . .

The author of the second article (author A), who is writing about the eMarketing firm Bookbub, wishes to remain anonymous. He has had four successful literary novels published mainstream over the last fifteen years, and has recently moved into alternative methods of publication. Sites like Bookbub are relatively new, and I've not yet used them, but the article has really made me very interested and I shall give them serious thought.

Bookbub eMarketing – Article by Author A

If your book is available digitally, through Amazon's KDP, Smashwords, or one of the other eBook retailers, and you are prepared to discount the book to 99p or 99 cents for a limited period (which may be around the 70p mark, depending on exchange rates) you may wish to consider a promotion site, like Bookbub, that email subscribers with special offers and tweets, and 'Facebook' their chosen titles. After all, there's no point discounting a book if nobody apart from your immediate circle of friends and readers is aware of the special offer. There is also only so much you can do yourself via social media to promote a sale. *(For information on how to discount, or lower prices, look up the Amazon KDP options – MC)*

Many promotional sites have sprung up in the last few years, that offer, for a price, to alert their subscribers to discounted eBooks. Unfortunately, for the debut, or still-to-be-widely-discovered author, the sites you'd most like to advertise with, are usually those most fussy about the titles they take. *Bookbub*, for instance offers discounted books by the likes of John Irvine and Nora Roberts, so to persuade them that your title merits inclusion in its emails and on its website, you need a strong offering. More thoughts are given on this below.

Many of these promotion sites operate out of the U.S. If you are a British author, this is great because the U.S. market is far larger than the British market. Many of them, including Bookbub, have British subscribers, too, so you can cover both markets.

A typical eBook promotion works like this. You choose a good date for a price discount (you may want to lower the price on your supernatural thriller to 99 cents over Hallowe'en, for instance) and either adjust the price yourself manually, or go through the KDP dashboard, to access the Select promotions available to you if your book is exclusive to Amazon. With this latter option, you might choose to run a Countdown promotion for five days, lowering the price on the first day to 99 cents and increasing it every day or so until it returns to its original price.

You then approach a promotional site. Assuming they accept your submission you pay them a sum that could be as little as $10 or as much as $700 to include your book sale in the daily (usually) email they send to subscribers, place the book on their website and tweet and 'Facebook' the special price. For the purposes of what follows we'll look at a Bookbub promotion assuming the following:

- You are offering a 99-cent self-published eBook (obviously you could be running a UK 99p promotion only or in conjunction with the U.S. promotion, but we will simplify the sums by sticking to dollar prices as Bookbub is American).
- The title is enrolled in the KDP Select program, thus retaining 70% royalty on the 99-cent discounted price as part of a Countdown promotion (outside a Select promotion, dropping the price to this level would place the title in the lower royalty bracket, obviously taking a big chunk out of returns).

Bookbub is undoubtedly expensive. It may cost $500-$700 to advertise a 99-cent historical fiction or mystery title. The high prices do, however, reflect the fact that average sales, as a result of a Bookbub promotion, can be 2,000-3,000+ (see their website for more indications of how many you are likely to sell for any genre/discount). It's worth noting that the site may not be able to take you on the exact date you offer, so be prepared to be flexible with timings. Authors sometimes combine a number of promotions over the life of a price drop – take care with your dates and double-check that Amazon has actually lowered the price when it is supposed to. Also be aware that if your UK price is pegged to the dollar exchange rate, a currency fluctuation could mean that your UK price changes without you being aware, or possibly vice versa. Sometimes KDP will refuse to allow a Countdown to go ahead because a price increase or drop has occurred within a certain timeframe – without you being aware of it. If you are dropping a price in the U.S., ask an American friend to check that the price is what it is supposed to be: you can't tell from this side of the Atlantic. Some of the promotion sites are very particular about a price discount happening at precisely the time you told them it would happen.

Assuming Bookbub accepts your book (and if so, well done! – pour yourself something celebratory) and the promotion runs, the figures might look like this on a 99-cent book: 2,500 sales @ 99 cents = $1,732.50 at 70% royalty. If you paid $700 for the promotion, you'd thus be over $1,000 up as a result of the promotion. Net returns will vary according to where you sell books – distributors have different royalties, so you'll probably need to spend some time with a calculator and/or Excel spreadsheet to work out what you're likely to make. It may be at one of these moments that you wonder whether being a writer was really meant to involve crunching figures. You may even want to return to the chapter in your WIP you left off writing because you were stuck.

It's more than just making money. Promoting your book is also about propelling a title up through the Amazon rankings (to be honest, despite the multitude of other distributors, Amazon still seems to matter most) and hopefully gaining more visibility for any other books you have published, too. Although the exact workings of Amazon's algorithms are a mystery, the site seems to work on the basis of *whosoever hath, to him shall be given, and he shall have more abundance.* The better a book does, the more attention Amazon gives it, for example, emailing it out to its customers as a suggested read.

Not all titles do equally well at Bookbub. The site includes a very useful blog, Bookbub Unbound, that tells writers what Bookbub subscribers really loved at various points during the year. At the time of writing, it is novels about family secrets. In the summer of 2014 it was historical fiction set in World War 2. The blog also provides useful graphs and charts showing the success of various genres and the demographics of Bookbub subscribers (providing even more worthy excuses for neglecting any actual writing you should really be doing).

In trying to get a book accepted for a promotion it is worth checking out the *Kboard Writers' Café* forum, where authors share the results of various eBook promotions, or express (more often) their utter frustration at not being able to gain a Bookbub slot for a title. Do not be dispirited if you fall into this category: many very talented writers have to apply several times before they succeed with Bookbub. That said, in all honesty, you will probably have less chance of inclusion in a Bookbub, or similarly well-regarded promotion, if you are a new writer of a single title with just two or three Amazon reviews. Rumours abound that Bookbub will only take you if you have a minimum number of reviews (fluctuating from about 10 to 100), but the truth is that authors have run Bookbub promotions with as few as 11 reviews on Amazon because there was something else about them, their title or their backlist that Bookbub knew would appeal to their subscribers.

Reviews are useful, however, even if it is irksome and time-consuming to persuade people to write them. Perhaps consider using *LibraryThing* and *Goodreads* for giveaways and/or offer the book to blog sites that review in your genre. If you have received prizes or nominations for your work be sure to highlight these, too, on your Amazon author page and website. Equally, if you have sold a lot on a previous title, either in the UK or overseas, this is something you need to push. If you are self-published, but previous titles were published by a traditional publisher, this is worth pointing out as it is a clear indication that publishing professionals considered you worthy of financial investment.

Of course, there are many other promotional sites other than Bookbub you should consider. Here is a short list of those often discussed online. Requirements and prices are correct as at July 2015, and are *for books discounted to 99 cents.* Many of the sites run a number of differently priced promotions for free books, or books priced at $1.99 or $2.99, for special placements. It goes without saying that all these sites all require professionally designed covers and properly formatted and edited content. (Do examine the websites and current deals from all the sites below, as things change very fast in the subscriber eBook fields – MC.)

Ebooksoda
Will take books, with a minimum of eight reviews and an average star rating of 3.5. Costs $10

The Fussy Librarian
Will take books with 10 reviews and an average star rating of 4.0, or 20 reviews and a 3.5 rating, with a split between the U.S. and UK. Costs $5-$14

Booksends
Will take books with at least five reviews, with a high overall average. Costs $10-$60

Ereader News Today

Does not specify number of reviews, but looks at them to get an idea 'of how well received' the book has been by readers. Costs: $15-$45.

BKnights
An operator on the Fiverr site who will promote your book via twitter/the BKnights website/email. No minimum number of reviews. Costs: $5-$20

Do your homework before parting with money. Be sure to research any promotional site thoroughly before you pay anything, preferably by going to writers' forums such as Kboards where people relate recent experiences. Some genres seem to do better with some promotion sites than others.

The methodology described above has been based around a 99-cent book. Rates will be cheaper on most sites for free books. Think carefully about offering a title for free, though. Not only will you fail to recoup advertising costs, you may just be giving your work away to people who might have paid for it. Free promotions do work well in certain cases: notably where an author has a new title out in a series, and offers the first book free as a hook to entice new readers into buying further works. Authors sometimes also use free books as a means of obtaining reviews on a title that is finding it hard to gain them organically. A word of caution here: you might think that readers would be well disposed towards a book they'd been given for free, but looking gift horses in the mouth is not unknown among Amazon reviewers, particularly where they have strayed away from genres they prefer because a title is free. And *keep researching the market.* Once again, do not take any of the above as Gospel. Trying to present a definitive guide to what is working in eBook promotion at any given time is like trying to jump off a motorway bridge onto a speeding Porsche! Good luck!

MC: Do check the criteria of eMarketing sites regularly as, being in direct competition with each other, they are always trying to encourage authors to 'use me'. For instance, The Fussy Librarian now allow your book to be included in more than one category at a generous discount

My eBook Success – Interview With eBook Author, Tim Stevens

Tim Stevens is a renowned and very successful eBook author. Despite his incredibly busy schedule as a family man, and a Consultant NHS Psychiatrist, he is the successful author of twelve action packed espionage eBooks. He has been described as '*one of the best writers of thrillers working today*', and '*the new master of the genre*'. His most successful works include *Ratcatcher, Omega Dog, Sigma Curse, Severance Kill,* and *Cronos Rising.* His sales exceed 5,000 per month and are rising fast.

Mary: Thank you very much, Tim, for agreeing to be interviewed. Have you always wanted to write, or did it just 'grab you' one day?

Tim: Always wanted to, from about the age of ten. I devoured Agatha Christie from the age of eight, and wrote my first murder mystery at eleven, as well as a couple of science fiction tales. The writing bug went away in my teens and early twenties, when other life priorities got in the way, but as I was pushing thirty I started to feel the urge again to write. Like many authors and would-be authors, I was 'working on a book' for about ten years, though I wasn't really doing much except thinking about it. What focused my mind, and my energies, was the imminent birth of my first child in late 2007. I realised that if I didn't knuckle down and actually *write* my book, while I still had a relatively big amount of free time, I never would. So I wrote my first novel – still unpublished – in three months, and started submitting it to agents soon afterwards.

Mary: Your output is phenomenal – a new eBook every six weeks or less – so I guess you have to fit in strict writing time every day. What is your regime?

Tim: I set myself a weekly word count and stick to it, managing to hit it most weeks. A daily word count is unrealistic, I've found, but that might vary from person to person. I usually write for half an hour in the morning, before the house descends into mayhem, and then for an hour to an hour-and-a-half in the evenings. I've trained myself to write quickly, and fairly cleanly, with a first pass so I usually manage an average of 3,000 words every day. It adds up, week on week.

Mary: Your sales are incredible, so readers of this book will be interested in finding out how you started your marketing and publicity campaign back at the beginning.

Tim: I did nothing! It was a chaotic mess to begin with. I did what most new independently published authors do: released my first book, convinced that it was going to be a bestseller, and waited for it to sell. It sold reasonably – a hundred copies the first month – but gradually tailed off. I started to tweet links to my book and post about it on Facebook, but I doubt I shifted many copies that way. Then I started researching the methods of successful self-published authors, and learned that regular publishing of new material is key. So I put nose to grindstone, or finger to keyboard anyway, and started working on the next book. It's only in the last six months or so that I've really kept up the output on a regular basis, and I've seen sales rise in tandem.

Mary: Do you now rely on your existing fan base, or try to 'reach out' to a new audience? If so, how do you do it?

Tim: Having an enthusiastic fan base certainly helps, and my mailing list is invaluable – I'd urge any new author to get one set up from the word go. But I do regular promotions using various online advertising services which puts my work in front of thousands of new readers interested in my genre. It's a constant process of promotion.

Mary: Do you use social media much, or are there other outlets within your specific genre?

Tim: I have a Facebook author page, but tend to post there when I have a new release out. The short answer is that I don't use social media very much to promote my work. I know many authors who employ it very successfully, but there's a knack to it which I haven't mastered yet.

Mary: Your books are marketed at very attractive prices. Are some of these 'special offers' or do you find that setting the price fairly low across the board is essential?

Tim: Low prices are definitely a factor in attracting new readers to take a chance on an unknown author. So most of my books are priced low enough they might be worth an impulse purchase, but not so cheaply that people might get suspicious as to why I'm offering them at bargain-basement prices. I do run regular promotions at 99c/77p on some books, particularly the first in a series. Also, I offer books free from time to time, as loss leaders to draw readers into the rest of the series. It's a strategy that's served me well, as it has lots of other authors.

Mary: It's obviously working as your sales figures are snowballing. Are you tempted to try and find a mainstream paperback publisher?

Tim: I wouldn't seek one out – I remember the months of agony waiting for replies which turned out to be rejection after rejection – but if I was approached, I'd certainly consider it. One thing I'd need to ensure is that I retained the eBook rights. Now, not many publishers offer this kind of arrangement, but there are some authors – Hugh Howey is the most prominent – who've successfully negotiated a deal like this.

Mary: Having heard about your literary creativity I'm fascinated with your C.V. Doctors are considered to be left-brained, yet authors tend to be right-brained. Did you have any career struggles?

Tim: The left/right-brain distinction is a bit of a contentious one, but if we assume it as a useful shorthand, I've always been more 'right-brain' than 'left-brain'. I had more of a natural aptitude for language than for the sciences at school. I suppose my choice of specialty – psychiatry – reflects this to some extent, though psychiatry is far more scientific nowadays than it's often portrayed.

Mary: What plans have you for your future writing life?

Tim: My goal is to go part-time in my job as a doctor, once my earnings allow it. This may be in one year's time, though of course this is an uncertain line of work and I'm not going to make any hasty decisions. But I'll continue to write, and aim to produce between eight and ten novels per year.

Mary: To conclude. Are there any other marketing and publicity tips you can give future eBook authors?

Tim: It's something I haven't tried, but there's good evidence that waiting until you have at least three novels ready for release before you publish the first one, seems to work wonders in many cases. Readers will often look more favourably on an author who has a few books available, and so you could hit the ground running with your first book.

Mary: Thank you again, Tim, for taking the time out to do this interview. (http://timstevensblog.wordpress.com)

The author of the next article (Author B) also wishes to remain anonymous. For most of his life he has been a business consultant, with a full and varied career. He has produced twelve crime genre novels, both as self-published paperbacks and as eBooks, and has sold several thousands in the Asian speaking countries, mid-west USA, and the home market.

Successful Alternative Publishing

All creative activities are subject to the filter of critical opinion and commercial considerations. It follows that success depends on getting one's work past these road-blocks and into the world. Going to Hollywood and putting up your stall as an actor or actress is a very chancy undertaking. The writer is hardly in a better position. One of the main difficulties lies in the huge level of competition in the marketplace. And why ever not as the rewards are great? A-listers, such as John Grisham and J. K. Rowling come to my immediate mind, but the motivation should be statistically realistic. Some writers speak frequently on the platforms of literary festivals and others paper their toilets with rejection letters.

Let us consider the life-cycle of a would-be writer. You have written your novel. You send it off to a literary agent. He suggest you send it to a literary consultancy (paid). This cycle repeats endlessly. You take advice and 'improve' your manuscript. Publishers put your work on the slush-pile or send it back unopened. Is it possible to win in this not very merry-go-round? Some do. Not many. Should you take up something else like table tennis?

You have a major decision to make if you are considering giving up on writing. To press on you have to make your own judgement about your work. The 'system' as described has rejected your work. Is your work complete junk in any reasonable terms or is it saleable commercially? To press on you have to accept that the only opinion that counts *is your own*. When you take that on board you have become a true writer. You have produced something that is unique to you and is a distillation of all you have gleaned from your unique passage through life, and now exists forever in its own right.

Where you go next depends very much on your true motivation. Do you want to make money? Do you want acclaim? Do you want to show your efforts for yourself alone, or for family and friends? Not a paltry ambition. A sensible person with forethought would have taken the Irish directions; you can't get there from here, and it came as no surprise to me when I reached this point.

My opportunity came with the first trickle of print-on-demand. I examined, with extreme scepticism, the offerings of almost every 'free' book-publishing offer. Although computer-savvy I found the interface with printing quite challenging. Page layouts, margins, cover pictures were OK, but only OK. I improved and I was encouraged to keep on going. I had been turned down by agents, consultants, publishers, every Tom, Dick and Harry. But my early paperbacks were fun, encouraging, and smooth in my hands. Anyone could buy them! Wheee!

It soon became obvious that they were selling well online, but I did not need my economics degree to understand that bookshop sales were not an option. Apart from the mark-down, there was the cost of trogging around the towns doing the unpleasant selling thing. But the world turns. Technology advances. Kindle and other eBook readers were launched, and Kindle made me an offer I could not refuse.

KDP (Kindle Direct Publishing) was something else, with tens of millions of Kindle eBook readers. Tens of millions of eNovels to potentially sell! I did the sums. First I had to sign onto a Kindle author's account. Then D-I-Y became more difficult as I had to convert my Word manuscript into Kindle language. But being computer-savvy I did not have to pay for all of this, and therefore (to me) cost-free. Cost-free? Yes! No printing costs, postage, or paper. Glub! I could set my own selling price (within significant constraints). If I was a famous, drooled-over, author I would receive maybe 7-10% of the *net* selling price but as a Kindle author I received 70% of the gross selling price, by direct debit, straight into my bank account,. I can promise you writers, it is a jolly good way to start the day over breakfast to receive an email telling me to look at my bank account 'cos they have sent some cash!

During my watch the Kindle eBooks market has slowly expanded, country by country. It certainly covers the Anglophone countries and a good chunk of the rest of the world who can read English. So. Now I have my dozen novels up on Kindle, how do I expedite matters so I can have my breakfast interrupted by financial matters? Well, I am part of the most-read genre category – crime. But this is more good luck than good management, knowing full well that my stuff (in terms of genre) would have the best chance of selling. That should not put you off doing what you do well. Writing is difficult enough without going off into left field chasing commercial success.

Marketing is usually refined by targeting particular segments of the population. Twittering, or Facebooking (or any such solecisms) is beyond my intellectual comfort zone, so in reality your novel has to stand or fall on its own merits. Some have gone viral from such a position. Mine have not, although I consider I'm doing extremely well. So far. All I have done is to direct possible readers to my titles. And keep everything crossed.

So how have I done that? You should try for a popular genre. Crime, especially murder, is always good for a laugh and has universal appeal. But even narrow fields of interest would have a readership. Africans, I am told, lap up mysteries. So there you are slap bang in the middle of, say, the horrible murder category in which you have categorised your little story to the Kindle Computer. First it must appeal with a tempting title, ensuring you say what it's about, an in-yer-face cover, and an opening to hook the reader, accessed by the Look Inside feature. Even more important (especially in Yorkshire where I was born) is 'how much is it?' The cheaper the better.

Now we come to 'key words'. This is a very important additional thing that can attract readers searching for 'something' to read on-line. Once in a category you can lead them into your novel via carefully chosen key words on the Kindle Computer. What are your readers looking for? Violence? Sex? Murder in particular way? All sounds sordid but you have to talk to their subconscious. I do keywords on (hopefully) a subtle level. When I received orders from India, and you know from the Kindle Computer where you are selling (my crossover novels do well in the Midwest) I added key words to tell of an Agatha Christie olde-worlde England like wot it used to be back in the rose-coloured images of the Raj. I then added Inspector Morse for other reasons. And so on. You get my point.

EBooks have huge potential as there are billions of readers in the world. A tiny fraction is all you need. It's likely you can, in some fashion, direct many of them towards your work, but in the end stand back, write your next novel, check your bank balance over breakfast and know, (like there are lots of planets like earth in the universe) somebody, somewhere, is frowning over your novels with his finger hovering over the 'buy' button.

To sum up

The advice you've read about above is 'straight from the horses' mouth' and it's obvious that the horses are all very different! Although you'll probably have ended up dizzy with information on the differing methods of eBook sales, take things easy by examining each author's strategies slowly. Yes – if it's a whole new world to you it sounds very complicated – but once you've taken some time to evaluate, and mastered the basics, you'll begin to understand what's involved, and what might work best for you.

Part Five:

The Importance of Sales Campaign Materials

Chapter 7 : What Exactly Are Sales Campaign Materials?

Circulating Printed Information

Sales campaign materials are printed productions, or abstracts, that are used to promote and showcase your work, and there are two types; those aimed at the inner industry to entice interest in your book, and those you'll use in your own personal sales campaign. Although the larger part of this section is aimed at paper printed versions I advise all eBook authors to read it, as any tips concerning the circulation of information will be useful.

Pre-Publication

In large mainstream publishing houses the production team are juggling a great many books at the same time, and trying to get pre-publication sales for them all. They'll do this by producing an Advanced Information Sheet (AI) and a Press Release (PR). These are a standard part of mainstream publishing, and are used to act as a magnet for your book within the industry.

Sadly, some of the smaller firms don't get pre-publication sales. With poorly paid skeleton staff, and/or an army of 'interns', there will be a high turnover of personnel who have no autonomy in making innovative decisions. In these cases pre-publication attention can be very poor, and I can never understand why these firms go to all the trouble of publishing your book and don't help to secure early sales. It's a huge disappointment to the author – especially those with little experience – but all you can do is to familiarise yourself with the many areas of personal publicity and marketing, covered later in detail.

My advice to these neglected authors, and the self-published, is to produce your own AI and PR. Although you won't have the means to circulate them early within the trade, they are an essential part of your publicity arsenal.

The Advance Information (AI) Sheet

The Advance Information (AI) sheet is a valuable selling tool that is circulated to anyone who'll be instrumental in moving your book through the trade, such as reps, distributers, stockists, and retailers (all detailed later in *Behind The Scenes of the Book Industry*). As ever, there will be shed loads of competition, so it should be as eye-catching and as bright as possible. It must include comprehensive ordering data, an image of the book cover, a concise clever paragraph that describes the book's content, the targeted audience, and the author's contact details, including any online platforms. It should only state the essential facts as the recipients will never wade through verbose, rambling details about the plot or characters. All they need to know is, 'why this book will sell and why they should stock it'.

Mainstream: A mainstream publisher *should* prepare the AI and send it out on your behalf. You may have no control over it, or even be sent a copy. Details will be included in the very full and showy catalogues that the wholesalers circulate monthly to bookshops, and whilst this sounds great, they're nearly the size of the old style telephone directories. Publishers also have to pay to include a cover picture (around £100), and one hopes they do, as without it there will be no hook to draw any attention. The importance of the AI should not be underestimated, but there's no point producing one *after* publication; the trade wants to know what's coming up on the market long in advance so they can make stocking and buying decisions.

The larger publishing houses also have the luxury of presenting their forthcoming season's catalogues in advance to the chain retailers' head offices, and it's here that decisions will be made as to which books they will carry as 'core stock'. This includes their front-of-store special offers, and which titles they showcase in the window. In addition, sales reps will be targeting bookshops directly, using the AI. The downside is that smaller publishers won't be able to provide a high profile sales push in the media and the trade, and all the celebrity, and established names will, by default, be shuffled to the front of the queue. Thus, an unknown author's chances of being picked up by influential booksellers is remote. What I'd advise you to do is get hold of your AI and use it as part of your own campaign to create some advance interest yourself.

Self-Published: If you're self-published, and have opted to take advantage of your service provider's publicity and marketing package, they may offer to send out an AI. Check how it will be distributed, and at the very least ensure it'll go to the retailers' stock buyers, the wholesalers, and library suppliers. Otherwise it'll be very difficult for you to distribute an AI to the trade yourself as the key buyers are notoriously difficult to contact, and they change with monotonous regularity.

The Press Release (PR)

A PR differs from the AI in that it aims to sell the book to the media and the press, hopefully to get articles, reviews, mentions, and any other type of publicity. A well-constructed PR is an essential part of early marketing, but it will *also be ongoing* throughout the lifetime of your book.

Mainstream: A mainstream publisher *should* allocate you a personal publicist who will write a rough draft, and then work with you on amendments and additions. With my first novel the publicity department wrote one for me, but it was so bland and weak I spent many agonising hours rewriting it to my own specification. I've discovered that many mainstream authors actually end up writing their own, so my advice is to offer to polish your own PR. It's rare they'll object as both parties have the same goal – to sell your book. If you find you're not being involved do check on progress with your publisher as I've heard that some of the smaller publishers don't produce one. In that case you obviously write your own (see below).

Self-Published: Again, if you're self-published, and have chosen to pay your service provider for a PR, then find out *exactly* what you're getting for your fee before you sign up. For instance, make sure you're not being given a standard template where 'one-size-fits-all'. Insist on a designated name to work with, and always ask for examples of what they've produced for other clients in the immediate past.

Writing Your Own PR

Yes – of course you *can* do it very well yourself, and use it copiously, but here is a *serious alert*! There are so many books being published the media is not really interested in the storyline itself (no matter how brilliant it might be) *but in the story around it*. How many times have you seen someone on chat shows, and the 'Breakfast' television slots, talking up their new book? The interview usually focuses on something other than the book itself: the story round its creation, something unique about the author, social or newsworthy issues in the content, or previous work being short-listed for a prize. They won't be interested in another boring talk-up describing, 'An exciting new novel by . . .' (who's she/he?) landing on their desk. In busy media/journalistic offices you can imagine how many bits of paper that arrive are glanced at and binned without consideration? Masses! We're *all* bombarded with far too much unsolicited information so try to find a new angle that the local media, or specialist magazines, will pick up. It'll need to achieve a highly professional presentation and say '*I'm special, so buy* **me**'.

The production should cover one side of A4 only with a word limit of 200. As with the AI it'll need a picture of the cover, the title, all contact and purchasing details, and your name boldly displayed in an attractive font. As said, the attention span of the person reading it will be *very* short and dismissive, so a clear colourful layout, brevity, and a decent font will help. Think laterally. Perhaps your novel deals with a social problem, political scheming, or a topical scandal; perhaps it deals with bereavement, divorce, and overcoming adversity? In the case of my third novel, *Who Was Angela Zendalic*, I compared it to *Call The Midwife*, *Philomena,* and the TV show *Long Lost Family.* My first novel, *The Crowded Bed,* starts with a GP murdering his father-in-law *because he can*! And that, in itself, conjures up another well-known true-life crime story . . .

Trying to create something on these lines takes thought and innovation, but the cleverest of you will hone in on something. My advice is to write a rough copy of any length. Then leave it, and keep going back to it, so you see it with fresh eyes. The first time you re-read it, pick out and mark keywords in bold. Every time you update it more keywords can be added, and any waffle gradually deleted. Its appeal will also be enhanced by some endorsements, mini reviews, flattering sound bites or clever 'one-liners' that you have picked up on the way to publication, always ensuring you state the source.

Other Essential Marketing Materials

Think about how you want to market the book, and although online marketing is considered to be essential (full details to follow) there's nothing better than a personal contact 'gift'. I use an online service called VistaPrint to produce really excellent personal calling cards, bookmarks, rack cards, or postcards. They're very good value for money, starting with an entry level and going up to full colour on both sides. Only buy what you can afford, but they are a marvellous way of putting information about your book in people's hands, and making the cover high profile. Flimsy flyers are very cheap and cheerful, but as most of us take one in the street out of politeness, and bin it straight away, a decent card will get more attention. Make sure you make them another 'mini PR' with as much information as possible about you, your book, and how they can buy a copy.

Part Six:

Those All Important Reviews

Chapter 8 : We All Want Good Reviews

Getting a Review

Good reviews are a huge boost to your sales campaign. When your book comes out there are so many areas to pursue, it's difficult to know where to start, but no matter where you start, you'll have a better foothold, and a higher degree of confidence, if you have at least one good review to back up your marketing and publicity campaign. As discussed with 'endorsements', it's better to have one from someone professional or prestigious, but if not, one that's honest and well written will suffice. These quotes below are the ones most bandied about in the book world:

'There's no such thing as a bad review', and *'It's not the content of the review that matters – it's the length.'*

I disagree with both of them. Who wants a bad review, even if you get column inches given to it? No one! But I agree that the bat and ball of altercation, such as you frequently get with the shortlists of major literary prizes, goes a long way towards cementing a title in people's minds. Long after the controversy has been forgotten (or in most part never read – only heard about) the title garners huge attention. This is fine for the big-hitters who will have a huge presence in bookshops, and an established fan base queuing up to buy it, but for the writer on the nursery slopes any adverse comments could be a disaster. However, if you do get a good review, and use it publically, you must never edit the text to enhance it, and always attribute it to its source. However, you can extract the most flattering sound bite, by including . . . before and after the quote.

Before I go into review ideas here is an amusing guide to 'review shorthand' which has been compiled by the best-selling author, Sarah Harrison, and although it's obviously just for fun, we can all see the tired old rhetoric.

Sarah Harrison's Guide to Review-Speak

• Enchanting: there's a dog in it.
• Heart-warming: a dog and a child.
• Heartrending: they die.
• Thoughtful: tedious.
• Thought-provoking: tedious and hectoring.
• Haunting: set in the past.
• Exotic: set abroad.
• Prize-winning: set in India.
• Perceptive: set in NW3.
• Epic: editor cowed by writer's reputation.
• From the pen of a master: same old, same old . . .
• In the tradition of: shamelessly derivative.
• Provocative: irritating.
• Spare and taut: under-researched.
• Richly detailed: over-researched.

Non-Fiction Writers

Getting that first review or endorsement will probably be easier for non-fiction. If you're writing on a specialist subject you may already have a wide circle of contacts, or interested parties. If the subject is fairly obscure your sales will only attract a niche readership, but you'll want them to hear about your work and snap up a copy. The actual readership may be larger than you think if you consider interest in other English speaking countries. Is there a senior figure in your chosen field who you could approach? The more respected the reviewer the more kudos it'll achieve, so think big. If that fails think of *someone* worthy who could possibly help you.

I will take as an example (a wholly invented title), *The History of The Harpsichord*. Which harpsichord players do you especially admire? Don't be intimidated by their reputation as they'll have a love of the subject and are likely to be very interested in your book, even though a larger part of the content will probably be known to them. An approach can be made through their agent, recording company, or any personal contact you find through their website, blog or Twitter account. A short pleasant approach is all you need. Send your press release, enlarge your background, and describe your book, but don't attempt to flatter them too profusely. Even by Googling *The Harpsichord* you may be inspired. When I did this 'Harpsichord Restorers' came up. What about choirs, classical music radio stations, and dedicated music magazines? What about a music college, or a musical society that lauds a composer, like Scarlatti, who uses the harpsichord greatly in his work. The possibilities, to those with innovation, are endless, and also remember that these sources are paramount in trying to *make sales as well*.

Fiction Writers

The above advice is also useful if you have a particular theme that might appeal to a niche readership, but for fiction writers in general you should approach someone from your 'genre', or type. They will be able to highlight your book's qualities with authority, be it romance, light comedy, political/corporate drama, sci-fi, clogs-and-shawls, fantasy, horror, erotica, crime, espionage or chick-lit. Writing for children and young adults (YA) also falls into several categories, and with historical settings find someone who has serious knowledge of the era so they can value its authenticity. If your friend's Auntie's neighbour has agreed to take it on, make sure he/she is familiar and comfortable with your type of work. Like most people my own reading choices are very subjective, and as I personally don't read sci-fi, fantasy, erotica, horror or chick-lit, I'd be as good as useless in these areas.

I am a 'mid-list' author and to the books trade this means that although my works are never likely to be raved-up best sellers, they're certainly commercially viable. I like to think that the term mid-list reflects my hours of concentrated thought and unique story line plotting, rather than a predictable formula of comfortable characters and the necessity for a 'happy ending'. With all of my books I've mostly had very positive reviews, but occasionally I find that my work is deemed to be a little too intense or 'street-wise' for some (I lay the blame on my characters!). This is par for the course for writers like myself, so if your work is 'bold and honest' be very careful that your reviewer is as savvy as you are.

There are also many social networking and book-related sites you can approach, such as GoodReads (www.goodreads.com), and online blogger reviewers (more later) where you can try to get reviews posted, and discussions started about your book.

For all writers, if you're lucky enough to get a positive response, send off a complimentary copy *poste haste*, with a short letter of thanks, but don't sit around on pins waiting for a stunning review to come back within days. They may never get back to you for a variety of reasons, time being the major one. It might just be the truth (and you have to accept the fact) that they didn't like it, and had no intention of tarnishing their reputation (and yours) by saying so. Yes – of course, it's happened to me, and it's very hard to accept, but the only thing to do is carry on using your innovation to think up some others to approach.

Most writers can get star-studded reviews from friends and family, but good reviews from strangers and professionals are treated as the Holy Grail – a public acknowledgement of your writing achievement – but if the review is unfavourable can you accept it with good grace? It's human nature that you can't! This is one of the risks of putting your work out in the public domain, and there's nothing you can do about it. The most important thing to remember is that any review will be a personal opinion of the merits of your book. They can be long and detailed, or merely a sound bite, and you must be prepared for any lukewarm responses, mild criticisms or real disappointments. It's horrible, I know, as you want every reader to enjoy your writing, but the old adage of 'horses for courses' usually applies and you'll learn to recognise the clever 'get-outs' that some reviewers use – like merely reprising the story line without offering one word of praise.

Reviews on Amazon

The concept of selling your books on Amazon is covered later in the sales section, but Amazon is the easiest place, by far, for your readers (both known to you or otherwise) to put up a review. A good Amazon 5* review tends to be highly coveted as a showcase for praise, and being your largest 'window on the world' any interested party will be able to access your work, and (most importantly) read those reviews. They'll also be able to follow links to your other publications and, if your book is signed up to the 'Look Inside' scheme, be able to read an excerpt. For self-publishers 'Look Inside' is usually provided, and should be discussed with your service provider. You should even check this with your mainstream publisher as one of my books was left without it for several weeks – the excuse being that 'the person responsible had left and nobody noticed'. Not good enough!

Never write your own reviews as this is hugely unprofessional. However, there's absolutely nothing wrong with asking people you know, who have read and enjoyed your book, to upload a review on Amazon for you, as nepotism never harmed anyone. It's a very simple procedure to follow through the 'create your own review' box, and all that's needed is an Amazon account and password. Once again, can I repeat, that any review posted must be truthful, accurate, and reflect the reader's opinion of the book, but beware! If a so-called friend gives you a mean 'star rating' (as per, it's happened to me) then quietly ask them to take it off, as it's very unsporting for them 'to be so honest', publically. You may also come across an anonymous review that attempts to do you down and it's a sad fact of life that some people (trolls) can be very nasty. Hopefully, your reviews, endorsements, and sound bites will be flattering and can be used profusely within your marketing campaign.

In general, increased attention *is* being paid to Amazon reviews, and I've often seen them used as cover quotes. But again, beware! Some local independent bookshops, who feel that Amazon is putting the squeeze on their margins, may not take it too kindly if you plaster the dreaded word in the marketing materials you're using in their store. And don't just think Amazon. The Book Depository, WHSmith, Waterstones and many other independents, also have websites where readers can post comments. Reviews will be visited again later on in the 'sales' sections, most especially with newspapers and magazines.

Reviews From BookBloggers

A BookBlogger is *an independent person* who takes it upon themselves, *for no financial reward whatsoever*, to post online reviews about books they've currently read. It's often an admiringly long list, and the most successful of them have a huge list of followers, and enjoy many 'hits' a day. Every BookBlogger has their own unique style, the posts are diverse and idiosyncratic, and you'll soon acquire your favourites. The majority of them also include animated accounts of the joys and frustrations of their personal and working lives, their social outings, and their current opinions of the arts and the media. Their reading output is amazing, and they really *do* become 'cyber-friends'. The biggest breaks of my literary career were made by BookBloggers, and without them I'd have got very meagre coverage in any sphere.

To find them Google 'BookBloggers', look on the sites of as many as you can find, and follow them for couple of weeks to get a feel of their reviews. Most of them list alternative sister sites as well, so you'll soon build up a long list of those who are 'out there'.

If you want to contact a BookBlogger, to suggest a review of your own work, they will require a submission in the same way as approaching anyone else in the media, so you'll need to make yourself, and your work, stand out. However, the better known ones have, over time, been overloaded with requests, and are now rather 'taken over' by publishers. As much as they would like to oblige they only have so much time in a day, but if you get a positive response don't take it as read that a stunning review will appear. They may find they don't have time after all, or just didn't like it enough. And yes, readers – once again, this has happened to me on quite a few occasions.

To get a personal perspective on BookBloggers, my sincere thanks go to Jo Barton who Bookblogs as *Jaffareadstoo,* with the help and assistance from her beautiful ginger cat, Jaffa. I asked her to describe why she writes the blog, the pleasure she gets out of it, and her policy on reviewing.

Jo Barton from *Jaffareadstoo*

I've always been a prolific reader and enjoy reviewing books, on line, in book forums, and also in magazines. In 2011, I decided to enter the world of online book blogging. Having conducted my own research amongst the blogging community, I realised that my blog needed its own unique selling point in order for it to stand out. Taking my bibliophilic ginger cat as inspiration, *Jaffareadstoo* was born, and a blog I thought no one would want to read has since gone on to have hundreds of thousands of views. Visitors to the blog come from all corners of the globe and I know from the comments they leave, both on the blog and on social media, that they like what they see.

I have an eclectic taste in literature, covering a whole range of genres, and with this in mind I consider books from all publishing sources. Established authors can sit comfortably alongside independently produced writers, just as e-copies can be read with as much enjoyment as physical copies. If the story appeals to me I will read it, although, realistically, I have to be selective and state in my review policy that I reserve the right to turn down books. My blog is not a commercial venture. I don't profit by it in monetary terms, nor do I accept any payment for the reviews I write. I still consider it a privilege to receive review books in the post. or by email, and I would never infringe on an author's copyright.

My aim is to make *Jaffareadstoo* a fun place to visit, which is why I try to make it as interesting as possible; hopefully creating a welcome environment in which book lovers can stop for a while and maybe take away inspiration for their next read.

Review rules and criteria can be found on my website, http://jaffareadstoo.blogspot.co.uk

Google Alerts

If you want to be alerted to any online reviews, or mentions of you and your book (and who isn't), you can sign up to www.google.co.uk/alerts, a facility that tracks any talk-up, and emails you with the info. Just sign up both your name and your book(s) to get useful feedback. It's very quick, easy, and free.

In conclusion: Approach anyone who you think might possibly help you to get your book reviewed or praised in any way. Be very grateful to those that do, but accept that there are some who promise you faithfully they will, but never get round to it. Although it's very disappointing it's another of life's little vagaries, and it really 'isn't cricket' to nag them.

The Joy of Getting a Good Review

My first ever review came to me unexpectedly and unsolicited, and it was the breakthrough I needed. About six weeks after the publication of *The Crowded Bed* an unknown library reader from Ipswich, emailed my publisher. Her review was passed to me and I can remember sitting quite stunned that someone had taken the trouble to contact me, and to praise my novel so highly.

The Crowded Bed actually got a review by Kate Saunders in *The Times*, but it was a very convoluted and fortuitous journey: an example of how Lady Luck can suddenly come up trumps. My central character in the book is a Jewish G.P, and in thinking ways to get the book reviewed I asked my publicist to send a copy to the well-known personality David Baddiel. David is Jewish, a best-selling author who, at the time, wrote a high profile literary column in the Saturday edition of *The Times*. I was hoping that it would appeal to him but the whole exercise misfired! When I opened my copy (Saturday, February 17th, 2007) I discovered that David had devoted the whole of his column to explaining why he was *not* going to give me a review, together with a cartoon depicting himself holding up my book. His reason given was that he didn't want to be seen as 'British Culture's token Mr Jew'. Fair enough, but I did get my title mentioned several times in the article, and to an audience of many thousands. After that I approached the literary editor and asked in a very low-key way, if I might, as a first-time author, be given a conventional review. I also sent her a copy of all my other good reviews, and she was kind enough to grant inclusion. A month later the Kate Saunders review appeared.

After this accolade I got a bit beyond myself. I sent copies to all the other broadsheet literary editors thinking, rather foolishly, that they would take an interest, but unfortunately lightning didn't strike twice. Every submission was completely ignored. Zilch.

This is another thing you must get used to. Success – failure – success – failure, and luck is a *huge* factor. Sometimes the most unexpected things reap rewards, and some things that hold great promise fall flat. People let you down all the time, but you just have to get over it. It's a fact of life, not only in the publishing world but in life itself, and it's best not to let your heart bleed; just move on to the next thing. However, if you don't try then I can guarantee you one thing – you won't get anywhere.

Part Seven:

Behind The Scenes of the Book Industry

Chapter 9 : It's Complicated!

The Convolutions of The Book Industry

Having had my fiction published by every method possible I presumed I'd absorbed, over time, a reasonable amount of knowledge about the books industry. I was happy enough to see that each book was listed on a wholesale site (to supply bookshops) and stocked with online retail outlets like Amazon and The Book Depository. It wasn't until I came to write this book that I realised how little I actually knew! It was only after some intense research that I have, at last, begun to understand its complexities.

The more research I did, the more complicated it became, and I was in danger of completely losing the thread at times. Even people I've spoken to in the industry say the same thing; it's as complicated as fairisle knitting, and when you drop a stitch you have the devil's own job to pull it back into position. In this section I've given only the basic facts, but it goes some way to explaining the convolutions of the books trade.

By now you'll know that your completed manuscript goes off to the publisher, or service provider, who formats it into a readable book form and arranges to have it printed. We will now go through the next stages of your book's journey to the hands of a reader, and firstly there has to be an official recording of the book, in the form of an ISBN number, and BookData registration.

ISBNs (International Standard Book Numbers)

Having an ISBN is not actually a legal requirement, but if you want to sell your book, or eBook, through the official recognised books trade it's an essential condition of trading. Having one means your book is listed on all trade databases, which is essential when your book is sold 'through the tills' or on any online retailer site. It consists of 13 digits, and will normally be found, together with its striped bar code, at the bottom of the back cover. When the barcode is scanned its unique information flashes up, concerning the title, the author, genre, price, and how to order, and bookshops often use it as part of stock management to scan books in and out of wholesale warehouses. Although books can share a title, no book shares an ISBN, and rules thereafter are that any large print version, or new version with text changes, need to have a second one issued.

The other requisite with ISBN's is the legal deposit of copies and the following strict rules apply:

'One copy is lodged with The British Library in Edinburgh, and that five other copies are sent to the Agent for the Legal Deposit Office in London. They will distribute them to the following libraries on your behalf: Bodleian Library (Oxford), University Library (Cambridge), National Library of Scotland, Library of Trinity College(Dublin), and National Library of Wales.

If you are publishing *completely independently* (see the sections Creating an on-line, Do-It-Yourself Production and Using a Print Only Firm) you will be responsible for delivering these books yourself.

All publishers, including service providers and eBook consultants, will provide a hassle free ISBN as part of your contract, and the name of 'publisher' will be that of your provider. However, for the self-published only, you're quite at liberty to create your own 'publishing company', by buying, registering, and using your own numbers. If you are operating as a group the same applies, but there has to be a named owner of the numbers. The Oxford Writers Group, operates its own publishing company, under the title of *OxPens*, for which I am the official registered 'owner' of the ISBN's.

ISBN's can be purchased from Nielsen's (www.isbn.nielsenbook.co.uk) and the current cost is £105.75 for ten numbers, the minimum you're obliged to buy. Thereafter your company name will be registered at your home address, or the address of the elected holding member. Here is a fictitious example of what's involved.

'Victorian Life in The Forest of Dean – Stories, Anecdotes and a Photographic History', written and compiled by Archie Andrews. Published by Cinderford Press. Illustrated Hardback. 200 pages. £18.99

The author, Archie Andrews, is newly retired, very fit, looking for a new interest in life, and can afford to take the gamble that he can sell his book himself. If he can pull it off he *will* make himself an excellent profit, with no cut to the middlemen along the way. It's a huge risk, but Archie is a confident sort of chap, and he won't end up in the poorhouse if it fails.

Books of this type need to be of very good quality and, as they contain lots of photographs, are not conducive to POD. Thus, he will use an established independent printing firm, inform them of the ISBN he will be using as 'Cinderford Press', and all details of the book will be registered on BookData (see below). You can, of course, use your own ISBN's with *any* version of printed work, from novels to textbooks, but always ask your service provider, or printing firm, as to what the frontispiece wording will be. Most of them will wish to have their name somewhere in the credits, and some may not be at all happy with this, so check it out.

Alert: As you can see, it's very easy for anyone to set themselves up as a 'publisher' so always make sure, if they advertise themselves as such, they have a proven track record and can guarantee to provide the benefits of a mainstream publisher, such as editing and free printing. Otherwise, they fall into the category of 'self-publisher'.

If you have no intention of officially going through bookshops, and decide not bother with an ISBN, this is perfectly acceptable, and here again is a *fictitious* example.

'*In Memory of The Bulstrode Family*, Publicans of *The Flying Fox*, Wychwood-in-the-Hedges, 1819 – 2015 by Nigel Bulstrode. Illustrated with original photographs. 60 pages. £7.99. All profits to St George's Hospice where the last incumbent, George Bulstrode, sadly died in the spring of 2014.'

Nigel Bulstrode, will have produced this book as a labour of love, and as inexpensively as possible, using an independent printer: a distinctly not-for-personal-profit book, and may be not much more than a well-produced pamphlet. The selling price will be pitched to ensure a basic return on his investment, and thereafter any small profits will go to the Hospice charity. As a memoir of a 'much loved' local family, there will be a very strong local interest, but it's unlikely that its market will be anything other than the area surrounding the village mentioned, or villagers who have moved away. Although an independent bookshop in the nearest county town might be happy to handle a few, it'll probably be offered for sale in local village shops, other pubs, church fetes, WI's and in the Hospice charity shop. There, is, of course, nothing to stop Nigel participating in a sales and marketing campaign locally, for which more will follow in the sales section. As with any charitable connection, Nigel will have to show proper accounts as 'non-profit making' for tax purposes.

Good luck to both Archie and Nigel, but most of you will be going down the traditional route, and accepting a given ISBN.

Bibliographic Data

I apologise if this section is a weary drag through something called bibliographic data, but it's as well to know the facts. Bibliographic Data is the lifeblood of the books trade, and without the correct information in place your book's success will be seriously diminished. It's a dull old subject, but very important – so read on!

There are two main providers of bibliographic data in the UK: Neilsen and Bowker, with Neilsen taking the largest share. They will register every book with an ISBN on a database called BookData, and this information is circulated within the many tentacles of the books trade. Inclusion on this database is sometimes sold to the self-publishing author as a 'big perk'. It isn't! If you have an ISBN it's a requirement of law, and just because your book is listed there's no guarantee it'll be noticed and hyped up by anyone. The real value to the small-time author is that your title is easily found 'on the system' by any retailer or other party who searches for it, using the ISBN. eBooks are also required to be logged and this will be done for you by your eBook producer, or yourself if you produce independently. Writers of children's books should also investigate www.bic.org.uk/8/children's books.

The Retail Price

In addition to the barcode, and ISBN, the back cover usually displays the retail price. These days some small publishers and self-publishers don't display it, so it's something else that should be checked out. The reason for this ambiguity is because, since 1997, there has been no agreed retail price index for books (covered later in Bookshop Sales) and thus large discounts can be negotiated. Most of the larger outlets, like Amazon and supermarkets, will have the financial clout to discount very strongly, and this has led to cut-throat competition in the books world. Waterstones and WHSmith sometimes offer in-store discounts, but the retail price will always be displayed somewhere, and a three-for-two deal is the best you'll get.

The next section will go some way in trying to explain the basics of the discount system.

How Your Book Is Distributed Through The Books Trade

Your officially registered and shiny new book is sent out into the world depending on the clout of your publisher, but with each book and publisher having highly individual criteria, each one is unique. The very large publishing houses employ their own sales reps (probably on commission) and the middle-range ones will go through a distributor (a paid salesman) who aims to sell copies to bookshops and trade wholesalers. The smaller companies, and the self-publishing firms, will send copies straight to a wholesaler (actually a stock warehouse). The *distributor* and *wholesaler* are what we call the middlemen (i.e. beneficiaries in the profit chain) and their joint commissions share anything from 65% to 75% off the cover price. In other words, publishers only end up with between 25% to 35% of the cover price on books they actually sell. The wholesalers then sell the books to the retailer at a profit, imposing their own hiked-up price. This is why powerful bulk buying outlets can negotiate better deals, and small independent bookshops are struggling to compete. With so many grabbing hands it can be irksome that the miniscule mainstream royalty rates seem terribly unfair to the author, but you have no choice but to accept the system. It's the way the trade operates, and will always do so.

It's here that self-published books can triumph. They don't suffer from the same swingeing trade discounts, and there's much more profit left for you. However, all stock agreements will be handled by your service provider, so make sure you're completely *au fait* with your books availability to retailers; it's certainly not a 'done deal' that your book's appearance on BookData will result in wholesalers holding stock.

Wholesale Distribution Warehouses

No matter what route your book follows, they all eventually end up in a wholesale warehouse. Here retailers and libraries can order in very easily from a central source, and the main firms are Gardners, Bertrams, Marston, Orca, Grantham and TBS; names you're unlikely to have heard of, but your book will be going through at least one of them. All authors should find out where their books will be held, and how the publisher monitors sales and stock. Gardners, for instance, are very user-friendly, and you can check your own stock by going to 'Our Range' on their website, and searching the 'quick ISBN/EAN search'. Other wholesalers may not offer this incredibly useful option, and my most recent one refuses to tell me what the stock figures for my mainstream books are. This means that when I arrange a sales push I don't know if any subsequent sales will be honoured without a long wait for replenished stocks. It's quite hopeless, and all I can do is ask my publisher to monitor stock figures. Even then, at the end of the day, I've still no idea what my stock figures are.

For anyone who wishes to research the wholesalers in detail here are their websites:

www.bertrams.com
www.gardners.com
www.granthambookservices.co.uk
www.marston.co.uk
www.orcabookservices.co.uk
www.thebookservice

Part Eight:

Marketing and Publicity: Setting Up The Foundation of Sales From Your Armchair

Chapter 10 : Creating a Buzz About Your Book

Word of Mouth

It's a truth universally acknowledged that 'word-of-mouth' is the most important factor that sells a book. For the new or little known writer this can work well on a local level, but getting the attention of readers nationwide is necessary, in order to give the mouths some words of recommendation.

The journalist Danuta Kean had this to say in a past edition of *The Author*, a quarterly magazine produced by The Society of Authors.

'For what I choose to call real publishing, word-of-mouth is a better judge of quality, and long-term cultural impact, than chart placing. But if good books cannot compete in shops, because of an over-supply of mass-market produce that has to be pushed because it's expensive to acquire, it becomes virtually impossible to create word-of-mouth'.

Danuta is talking about quality publishing being inevitably forced to compete alongside the previously mentioned populist and celebrity publications, so what chance does the small author have? The only answer is to apply yourself to a concerted publicity and marketing campaign.

Nothing can equal the pleasure of holding your completed book in your hands, and seeing your name emblazoned on the front cover, but despite the euphoria, this is where the hard work begins. The advice I give to everyone (no matter what method of publishing has been used, including eBookers) is the same; if you're prepared to work hard, and with vision, you *can* make excellent sales. Try to create your own 'buzz', be as pro-active as possible, and do everything you can to bring your book to the attention of readers.

At the beginning of my publishing career I knew nothing – and I really do mean nothing at all – about the skills and knowledge necessary to become my own publicity and marketing manager. I thought I'd merely sail into every bookshop and library in the country and find my book on the shelves. Ha! That's fairyland. Like many authors I'd been so neurotically obsessed with getting into print it hadn't occurred to me how much I'd have to get involved with the sales side. When I discovered what reality was I was determined not to let any possibility pass me by through a lack of effort. At times I must have seemed manically driven, but I was determined to act upon every idea.

The biggest factor in selling your book is *you*, and your innovative skills. We all have differing personalities – from bombastic to painfully shy – and there's no way anyone can give you a blueprint for toning yourself down or boosting yourself up. I like to think (as does everyone!) that I sit somewhere in the middle; that I'm pleasant and articulate, and I come across as charming and courteous. My natural persona generally works in my favour, but occasionally I come up against someone who clearly can't stand me, and is determined to humiliate me, so be prepared for the brush-off.

Mainstream authors will be under pressure from their publishing houses to show early results, but the self-published have a great advantage; you're wholly in charge and not being bullied (or let down) by anyone. Your book doesn't have to be treated as a publishing pop song that has to sell multiple copies in the first five minutes or it's deemed a flop. You can concentrate on building up strong sales long after publication (known as 'the long-tail' effect), and it won't matter a jot if your sales are initially small. A 'tortoise and hare' philosophy means you can manage your campaign on a 'one thing at a time' basis. Small sales grow gradually and you get there in the end.

The following chapters will now go through a long list of practical methods that all authors can implement to try and get a firm base in a sales campaign.

Chapter 11 : The Internet and Social Networking

Using Social Media Platforms

Generally speaking, it's an 'age thing'. Schoolchildren and young people have been brought up with modern technology, use it as part of their everyday life, and probably get withdrawal symptoms if they're denied access for more than five minutes. Those of you under forty will probably use them regularly in some form, and the older generation can largely do without them! So. If you're not one of the converted, then you're going to have to find out what's involved, and use them to the best of your ability.

Social platforms are considered by publishers to be an absolute must in your quest to publicise your book, but . . . the big question is, do they actually help to boost your sales? Many of my fellow authors are sure they do, and are so dedicated they become a little neurotic about it. Some think not – that it's tedious, and trivial, and isn't worth the time you have to dedicate to it. Whatever the truth of the matter, *we are told that this is what we have to do*. Some of you will revel in projecting yourselves out into the ether to an audience of strangers, and enjoy the returning interaction, whilst others find it a confounded and invasive nuisance. However, with The Internet being unsurpassed in providing instant information, or for doing armchair shopping, your book *must* have a strong online presence.

Initially, every author, whether mainstream or self-published, must be urged to join the main two, Facebook and Twitter, in order to 'make that buzz'. *Not*, I hasten to add, about your *magnum opus* (where have you heard that before?) but about yourself, your thoughts, and your daily life! What, one will ask, is the point? The reason is that bombarding people with an avalanche of 'buy-my-book' information will make them thoroughly sick of you, but if you create an online presence about yourself you're much more likely to get 'friends' or 'followers'.

I'm only aiming to give a flavour of what can be achieved, so here are the basics in using social networking as a marketing and publicity tool.

Twitter

My husband's view of Twitter is that it's full of twits, tweeting other twits. Many people may think that, but it's not. It's full of people with out-reaching personalities who like to interact with a large community of fellow Twitters, and even the establishment use it these days. If truth be known I'm not a huge fan, but I do like to use social messaging to my advantage.

For the uninitiated (and there must be many) Twitter involves short messages, or tweets, in no more than 140 letters, that are sent out to your 'followers', but with being only short sound bites you have to be concise and creative. An account is very easy to set up, and it's so simple even I managed to do it myself. Search your browser for www.twitter.com, pick a password, a catchy username, and you're off. Your short 'profile' should include the title of your book to make sure you establish yourself as part of the literary world.

The best way to get started is to tweet your circle of friends and family with a, 'Hi, here I am, your novelist/writer friend' type message, and ask them to re-tweet it to their followers. Start following fellow writers in your genre, and if you follow *their* followers it's likely they will follow you back. This will generate your name being circulated in many areas and over time should result in an endless daily stream of returned comments, messages, alerts, tweets and re-tweets. Some people find this exciting (a great deal, judging by the amount of people glued to their phones) but for me I find there isn't the hours in the day to read them all. However, if you want to maintain a 'presence' then you have to keep it up. Your followers will expect replies, and many authors I know post thirty or forty times a day with what I term an addict's need; they just can't seem to let a minute go by without checking out their contacts and sending out fresh trivia. Thus, you *have* to like this sort of connection or there's no point in doing it.

A special feature called Tweet Deck can be easily downloaded; a dashboard of columns to arrange your 'response messages' in specific categories such as Friends, Mentions, Direct Messages, and New Followers. Also, if you have posted up something particularly interesting you can alert your followers, with personal messages to re-tweet the info. For help with using Twitter, there are many entry-level books to be found on Amazon.

Facebook

As with Twitter, joining Facebook is incredibly easy, and online directions are very simple. Once up and running you write your message (no length restrictions apply), bang on 'return' and your message is posted. This system uses 'friends' and as you enlarge your database you'll find you're magically given suggestions as to who you might want to link up with, and an email will alert you when your friends have posted news. Having just a few known friends will not be enough; you need to interact regularly and widely to have the best chance of making it work for you and (just as in real life) the better you are at social events the better known you become online. Thus, from a marketing point of view, you need to create as large a community of interested people as possible.

It's worth mentioning that if some of your 'friends' are other authors, it's been proved they're not the best at actually buying your books (being much more interested in their own projections). Their presence might not actually translate into sales, and they'll take up alot of your time.

Chapter 12 : Personal Websites and Blogs (Weblogs)

Setting Up A Website

Some of you may feel confident you can design your own website as online technology is making it ever simpler to design and run them. However, you'll need to know how they're created, understand 'programming languages', and the concept of hosting and servers. If you're not confident then getting a professional on board is the answer. Many operatives advertise their services online, and I advise that you find someone fairly local so they can visit you, and vice-versa. Yes, it's going to cost you, and you will have to ensure that your 'domain name' is renewed and protected annually, but it's necessary in a very competitive field. Whatever method you choose, it's a good idea to get a website set up fairly early on in the publishing process, so the web address can be put in the book itself, and on all your marketing materials.

To a professional the technical setting-up procedure is straightforward, but *you* must have some idea of what you want the design and layout to be, and provide all the essential text. Clarity is the order of the day, as a dull, badly designed website will actually turn your viewers off. Actually, when researching this topic for *Calling All Authors*, I found that nine-tenths of sites I visited were too congested, too fussy, and too difficult to negotiate. So, as with book covers, look up the sites of several famous authors and decide which ones are the most appealing, and what puts you off. What colours do you like? What headings do you want? What fonts are easy to read? How many sections will you need? Make sure it's easy to navigate, with attractive, decent size fonts, and be pleasing to the eye. Be prepared to be guided by your designer as well, as he/she is in the business to do a first class job, will be keen to maintain a reputation, and won't be happy with a substandard production.

You'll also need to give some thought as to what you want your website to achieve. I would say that most authors want one that gives good information about their book(s), lively details about themselves (including photographs), bold images of the book cover(s), and all bibliographic data. Sample chapters should be made available similar to the '*Look Inside*' feature on Amazon: if the reader hasn't heard of you they may be hesitant about taking a risk and will appreciate the chance to read a sample first. Make use of every sales opportunity by linking to Amazon and other downloads, through a 'one click', facility that goes straight to instant purchase. Once the site is up and running, it can't be changed or added to very easily, so you may want to incorporate a built-in news feature you can edit yourself, or use a blog (discussed next).

Getting Your Website Noticed

Apart from putting your website address on every piece of promotional material you produce, what more can you do to get your work noticed online? One universally used method is to get your details picked up by search engines, such as Google, Ask Jeeves, and Mozilla Firefox, by using Search Engine Optimisation (SEO); a process whereby 'key words' are flagged up. Discuss this with your web designer for any free schemes, or look up *Search Engine Optimisation* for more information. Choosing appropriate words isn't easy, but (as with the advice on the eBook section) it's worth spending some time on it. Another option is joining a scheme such as AdWords (www.adwords.google.co.uk), one of Google's advertising methods, also based on key words that people search for. Adwords is quick and fast to sign up but it's expensive, and you have to decide, right at the beginning, how much your daily 'spend' will be; a serious budgetary consideration.

Networking via 'A Blog'

Once your website is up and running it's difficult to tinker with, but an excellent 'other' or 'extra' is a blog (weblog). If you don't want to pay out for a website, a blog is an excellent free alternative, and a great way to interact online. Examples are *blogspot* and *typepad*, and it's also possible to have one incorporated within your website. A blog can be a great marketing tool, with a facility to post articles and photographs, and setting one up takes very little time. It's a great place to put up all your news and happenings, and any outdated postings can be easily removed. There are many types of design, colours, and fonts to choose from to make your site unique, so they're not all just carbon copies of each other.

Many authors use their blog as a daily diary of what's happening to them in their writing life, such as events and talks they're doing, and regular views on all things literary. By making sure you add your blog address on all publicity materials, you'll gradually find you have regular visitors. These numbers can be tracked and will inform you of how many 'hits' you've had. As with all social networking you'll need to cultivate a following to get the most out of it, and ideally you want to attract an interactive bunch who'll post comments. I personally ran a very lively blog for three years, but gradually found the novelty was wearing off and I was tired of keeping it going. Thus, I don't blog anymore, but I really would advise you to try one, at least to see if you have the energy for it. (StopPress: I've decided to revive it!)

If you do start, then it's essential you keep it up, as many of your followers will expect some regular info. Some authors post daily, but ensure you put something up at least once a week as there's little point in being half-hearted. Never post out too much personal information or 'controversial gossipy chat' that might cause you to be targeted in any way (nasty trolls again). Also be aware of the 'comments' section as you can pick up messages from some very weird sources (I got alot). Don't respond to anything that looks dodgy, and make sure you're properly 'locked down' and protected security wise. Another tip is to try to link up with other author bloggers by interviewing them on what is called a 'blog tour', or inviting them to post one-off articles.

Forming a Collective Authors' Blog

How about starting a 'collective authors blog'. If you and a lively set of author friends can agree to post regular and lively articles, about anything to do with books and literature, you could soon attract a following. I've been a guest blogger on a site called Authors Electric (authorselectric.blogspot.com); where thirty authors from varying backgrounds, each post regular daily interest features on a variety of topics. With around 300 hits a day you can see that a collective blog is great place to be 'seen'.

Using Social Media Effectively

I'd now like to introduce you to a very successful author, Marissa de Luna, who has kindly agreed to be interviewed on how she uses social media. Her first novel, *Goa Traffic*, was self-published and her second, *The Bittersweet Vine*, mainstream published with Thames River Press. She is in her early thirties, and has just published the first of a cosy crime series, '*Under The Cocoanut Tree*, featuring a Goan detective, Inspector Chupplejeep. All her books are available on Amazon as eBooks and paperbacks. I'm sure you'll find this 'in a nutshell' advice useful from an extremely dynamic and brilliant self-publicist.

How I Use Social Media (SM) – Interview with Marissa de Luna

Mary: Hi, Marissa. Thank you so much for offering to share your Social Media skills. Can I first ask you why you use this method?

Marissa: As an author I like nothing more than completing a book and starting on the next. And if I'm honest, spending time publicising my existing novels doesn't appeal to me. I would rather spend time working on my next manuscript. However, I know I need to connect with my readers, not only to make sales but to keep in touch with what readers want. Additionally, social media allows me to reach my audience without breaking the bank.

Since self-publishing *Goa Traffic*, and having *The Bittersweet Vine* published by mainstream Thames River Press, I have realised the importance of SM. Through my own research on the do's and don'ts of SM, but mainly trial and error, I have picked up some useful tips and am happy to share them with you. SM is a cheap form of advertising, but remember that it takes valuable nuggets of your time. And if you rely on writing for your main income then this will detract from your writing time. But I have realised that the more you put in to social media, the more you will get out of it.

There are several reasons you have to get involved with SM including 'brand awareness' for your author name, direct publicity for your book (which ultimately should lead to sales), and increasing word-of-mouth publicity – the very best publicity there is.

Mary: What are the various platforms you use?

Marissa: There are hundreds of forms of SM (some of them have already been outlined in your text) but my comments only relate to the ones I personally use. They are: Facebook (FB), Twitter, Blogger, GooglePlus (similar to FB), and Linked-In, a professional networking site that has some great groups for authors, and where I have had the most engagements and blog views.

Also, I use Good Reads, a book review site where you put books you have read, or are going to read, on virtual shelves. Here you can have an author profile linked to your books, conduct book giveaways, and join forums and groups all about books. Another is Pinterest where you create a profile and pin pictures to virtual 'pin boards'. I have an author board, a writing board, a book marketing board, and a board for each of my books and works-in-progress.

Mary: Is it important to find out who your SM supporters are?

Marissa: Yes it is, so you can keep contacts buoyant. Okay, so you've sent a tweet and put a post on FB. Look at who retweets (RT) you and who 'likes', or shares your FB status update? Gather data on who these people are and return the favour. Listen to what they have to say and target them. If it's something specific they support about you, ensure they get your news messages related to what they are interested in so they can re-distribute the message to their own audiences. Yes! They will act as your mouthpiece, and promotion is always better when it *doesn't* come directly from you. Why? Because it is more believable. Also, this breeds word-of-mouth advertising which is crucial to building your brand/exposure, your popularity, and ultimately your sales.

Make friends with other authors you meet in the virtual world of Twitter. Two successful authors I met on Twitter have helped me in the past. One author wrote a guest post on my blog, and another hosted part of my 'blog tour'. Instantly I was reaching out to a whole new audience. In this way you can create your own little SM community. You'll also have a set of like-minded people or a bunch of readers you can call upon when you need to for their opinions.

Remember to start conversations. Don't just talk *at* people. If you met someone in the street would you just go on at them about your book's latest five star review? No. So read their posts, respond to their queries, always respond to direct questions – it's rude not to – and ask questions. It doesn't all have to be about writing and your book.

Mary: Is it important to try to make yourself personable?

Marissa: Absolutely! Be yourself. Readers will buy your books if they like *you* so don't be a one-dimensional character, and think about how characterisation works. You need to be well-rounded for people to like you and therefore find your 'voice.' People want to hear what you have to say, and again you know about this skill from writing. You need readers to like you and be your supporter. You can only do this if you are authentic and genuine. Don't talk about yourself incessantly, and don't be pompous.

Mary: I've heard that some novelists create platforms for their characters.

Marissa: This is a really good idea and I will be doing this for the central character from my new detective novel, *Under The Coconut Tree,* concerning A. Chupplejeep, a Goan detective. Create a Twitter Account/Facebook page etc in the name of your protagonist and use their voice. Post things they would like to say, and speak *as them.* As writers we all want to get inside our character's heads and this will kill two birds with one stone.

Mary: Can you suggest some Website tips?

Marissa: A website is a very important tool for improving your online presence. I believe that building a 'web presence' over the last couple of years has improved my book sales. It's like having a shop front and adds to your credibility. Have a look at other authors websites for inspiration and don't be afraid. Websites are easier to set up than you think and many companies, like Go Daddy, offer a full package with templates for web building as well. Another thing I add to my website is 'widgets' (bits of HTML computer speak) which add buttons and logos that display your SM sites so they can follow you there. A handy tool to use on your website is *Google Analytics.* This software is free and will enable you to track where your audience is coming from, and how long they stay on each webpage etc.

Mary: You can also link up your platforms, can't you?

Marissa: You can, using something called Hootsuite, a Social Media Management Service. This allows you to access all your SM outlets on one website. You can therefore log into Hootsuite and provide updates, as opposed to logging into to each account separately. Hootsuite also allows you to analyse your content and your audience, helping you to be one step ahead when getting to know who your supporters are. You can also use *Twitterfeed* so that every time you post a blog it automatically puts a link on Twitter, and links your Good Reads account to your blog posts so they show up on your page and your Google Plus account.

However, before you link-up all your SM platforms think about your audience. Your followers on Twitter may be different to those who visit your blog, so think about whether you want to send the same message to both platforms. Would you send the same query letter to four different agents? Personally, I don't link my Facebook page to my blog or twitter. I just add updates and links manually and post my blog updates on Goodreads, Google + and Twitter. It is time consuming, but I feel more in control of the content this way.

Mary: Putting yourself out in the media can lead to controversy. How should you deal with this?

Marissa: In all your media dealing be a lover, not a fighter. You will get a few adverse tweets, comments, or reviews and my advice is this: Don't try to defend yourself. Not everyone will like what you have to say and you have to respect that. If you don't, it will just become ugly and will put people off your brand. So remember, whatever you post, think first as to whether you want to be known as the author who said . . .

Although you shouldn't snap back at critics you should declare your own opinions. In fact being opinionated will get you more followers and engagements. People don't want to follow someone who just sits on fence all the time. I haven't managed yet to create a controversial stir, but I am sure some people are great at this without being hugely offensive. Remember, people want to hear your voice, so speak up! If someone has taken time to engage with you, respect what they have to say, even if you don't always like it.

Mary: A media presence can be an excellent way of knowledge sharing, can't it?

Marissa: Yes. Be the jewel in the crown, and by this I mean give back and add value to your audience. For example on my blog (http://thecoffeestainedmanuscript.blogspot.com) I have an *'In a Nutshell'* series where I write about different tips I've picked up in regards to developing my writing skills. I created it quite simply to give back. I'm not an authority on everything and initially I thought I didn't really think I knew enough to pass it on, via a blog, but now I just roll with it. I put my thoughts out there because they may help someone, or provide entertainment at least and it's giving back. Forums can be very useful and they are not *old skool*! I once thought this, but it's not true. Log on to writing forums like Wattpad and Writing Forums and get chatting. Commenting and talking on any public platform leads to interaction and engagement. You need people to take notice of you, so think of it like a hook in the first chapter of your novel.

Mary: How would you advise a new author to start?

Marissa: When you are just starting out don't spread yourself too thinly, so it's best to pick one or two sites to get involved with first. Once you are set up don't let your accounts gather virtual dust. You need to utilise them to your advantage. If you don't use them often enough, readers will lose interest and all the work you have put into creating your author brand will have been a waste of time.

I suggest new authors start with a blog. Although it can be labour intensive, it will help you keep your writing fresh. It will also give you a platform to let off steam. Try and blog every day, little and often, about anything that takes your fancy. You can also use Blogger to schedule posts in the future which will help with managing your time. Write five in one sitting and drip-feed them out. Twitter is another good form of SM to start with. It's not my favourite form of SM but it gets you out there. With Twitter I'm told one should tweet 7 times a day to get noticed, so keep the content of your SM fresh and relevant to stay in people's minds. From there on, you can get involved with other SM platforms.

Mary: And finally?

Marissa: Don't expect all this hard work to immediately correlate into sales! You have to be continual in your social media postings and be patient. But remember that with every tweet, post, 'like' and share you are creating a brand for yourself. So that's all from me. I hope you have found this useful. You can find me on:

http://thecoffeestainedmanuscript.blogspot.com,
twitter : @marissadeluna,
facebook.com/marissadelunaauthor,
Pinterest: Marissa de Luna

Mary: Many thanks, Marissa, for sharing all this valuable information. I'm sure that readers will now go forward to using SM platforms with every confidence.

Chapter 13 : Approaching Newspapers and Magazines

The Current Climate in Media Publishing

Having prepared excellent marketing materials, trying to get an early review, and setting up social platforms, the next stage is to get some media coverage. There are two types to try for; a review or a feature. The recession, and the huge growth of online information, has meant that sales of newspapers and magazines have greatly diminished. Many literary editors and reviewers have disappeared, but try to seek out the survivors, as this type of publicity can make a name for both you and your book. Before you go 'cold-calling' try approaching anyone you know who works in the field of journalism. If you don't know anyone (and most of us don't) ask around to see if your friends or acquaintances have any contacts. They may be kind enough to put a word in for you, so don't be shy of nepotism.

Start Small

Getting into newspapers and magazines, both local and national, is a mixture of luck, perseverance and damned hard work. Mainstream authors might possibly have had the input of a publicist to pave the way, but there's no guarantee of acceptance, and most of you will be representing yourselves. The idea, of course, is to get your work publicised, and hopefully make sales, so a good idea is to start small. There must be hundreds of people who live in your area, and many of them will know you, so how about a flyer/article in your parish newsletter, village magazine, any social organisations, local bookshops, or any other pick-up point, like community centres, corner shops, and your place of work.

Widening the Net

Now move on to bigger things. *The Writers and Artists Year Book* lists every newspaper and magazine available in the UK and Ireland, and a good starting point is to make out two separate lists; one headed '*might have a chance*' and the other '*stands little chance*'.

The first list is most likely to include regional and local newspapers, but due to falling sales across the board, many are being forced to operate on a reduced basis, or have closed altogether. However, those who have disappeared in paper form usually provide an online presence, so investigate fully. Generally, most of the survivors will still have a small review column, or a weekly arts page, but (sadly) due to diminished column space, being a local author isn't the door opener it used to be. As outlined in the section on *Writing a Press Release*, features editors will be far more interested in 'what you've done', so try to be creative and find a reason why the spotlight should shine on *you*. Fiction writers can make this work by hitting on an all-important 'hook', but non-fiction writers may find it a little easier if the subject matter is extremely interesting or topical. A (fictitious) title like *Facing Poverty – How To Eat Healthily on Twenty Quid a Week*, for instance, would be of great general interest, so get familiar with the publications you want to target, and look out for staff writers who cover areas relevant to your book.

Presenting a Sales Pitch to Newspapers and Magazine Editors

In making an approach you'll be fighting your way into a very competitive field, and every features editor, from the mighty to the small, is snowed under with begging letters, so first impressions are very important. Phone calls give a personal touch and can be more productive than post or email, but it takes great courage. Results probably depend on who you speak to on the day, and what sort of mood they're in. If they *do* say 'send in a submission' try not to get too excited. It may just be the usual busy-office shorthand to politely get rid of you.

Never just send a pack off 'blind' and hope for the best. A personal contact name is essential as it adds extra leverage when another member of staff, or temp, opens the envelope. A first class submission is essential in the same way as approaching agents and publishers but (as ever) *make it short*. With journalists being pared to the bone their time will be at a premium. One local journalist even advised me to present my own 'ready-made' article (with my photograph and an image of the cover), as this does all their work for them.

Always staple a compliments slip/contact details within your review copy in case the covering letter and the book become separated – highly likely in a busy office – and enclose a stamped, addressed envelope for return. Sending a complimentary review copy is very expensive, and you might as well get your investment back, even if you find it arrives back by return of post! If phone contacts don't come up trumps then send a friendly, lively email, without any grovelling.

Another idea is to actually exploit any geographical regions appropriate to your book. *The Priest, His Lady, and The Drowned Child* is set in Suffolk, and thus I was able to target publications especially produced for East Anglia. How about a special theme you could link in with. *The Crowded Bed* features a strong Jewish character and storyline, and (rising above David Baddiel's re-buff previously detailed) I managed to get a small review in *The Jewish Chronicle*.

The 'stands-little-chance' list (if you're being realistic) will be the broadsheets. Even *their* book reviews and features have sadly diminished, and what remains is largely showcasing authors the major publishers are pushing. All deny they 'pay' but it's certainly an elite crowd who gets attention. But anything's worth a go if you're really energetic. Another consideration is the pull-out magazine supplements provided in weekend editions.

The same serious contractions also apply to glossy magazines, but as a diverse list still remains, why not have a go? Serious fiction will have no place in women's or tabloid type magazines, and rompy romance is inappropriate to (for example) *The Spectator*. Always check that a book review section still exits, as I've discovered some don't have them any more (shame on them). If they do, try and research into back copies to see what the general selection includes to weigh up your book's suitability. Are all the reviews showcasing the big names, or do they occasionally feature an unknown with a small publisher? Do they feature both fiction and non-fiction, and is the selection eclectic? Would your book be too highbrow or lowbrow? Non-fiction writers – or writers in genres such as sci-fi and horror – have the added bonus of 'fanzines' which are specialist magazines and periodicals that might tie in with your topic.

For the self-published only, there is a dedicated magazine that reviews *only* self-published books: *The Self-Publishing Magazine* (www.selfpublishingmagazine.co.uk). This will include both paperback and eBookers, and is available by subscription only. By requesting a sample magazine you'll be able to decide if you wish to subscribe.

Also worth investigating are the publications that help and encourage writers, such as *The Writer, Mslexia, Writers Online* and *Writers' Forum*. It's unlikely you'll get any sort of publicity, but if you sift through all their advice and guidance you may find some inspirational ideas.

After every contact you make to *anyone*, tick the name off on your list, with a memo of whom you've spoken to, what you have sent, and the date (including rejections). If you don't you'll get yourself in a real mess trying to remember who came up trumps and who wasn't interested (a great failing of mine). Once the submission has been despatched and ticked, forget about it and move on.

After about a month you *might* follow up your request with a polite phone call, but don't be surprised if they can't recall either you or your book. This is *not* a damning negation – merely the result of their heavy workload. The name of the game is perseverance, and if you're lucky enough to get a slot, remember that you can quote extracts in your marketing materials and on your website. And don't let your ambitions stop at the home market. The world is your oyster, so when you've run out of options in the UK extend your horizons by searching online for potential targets in other English speaking countries.

To conclude: the world of journalism and the media is generally very hard to break into. It takes a great deal of time and effort, but if it works, it's the one sphere of publicity and marketing that can be the most useful and far-reaching in stimulating word-of-mouth.

Part Nine:

Book Sales on Amazon

Chapter 14 : The Value of Amazon To The Author

Paperback Sales

Whilst this section is dedicated to Amazon, as the front-runner of online book retail sites, there are many others, such as The Book Depository, Play.com, Books Online, Lovereading, WHS Online and Waterstones.com. However, Amazon have a near monopoly and definitely hold the biggest influence. However, these days Amazon are *not* the cheapest provider of paperbacks as they have removed their free delivery service on anything under ten pounds, which your book is likely to be. I guess the reason is to get you to sign up for Amazon Prime; a scheme whereby you pay £70 a year and have every purchase delivered free. Thus, suss out the smaller ones and make sure you mention where the best deal is to be had, anywhere you can.

However, for authors, Amazon does have some amazing perks. They are often portrayed as the big bad bully boy of publishing, being criticised for pushing independent bookshops out of business, and for being heavy-handed in demanding (and getting) the largest discounts around, currently about 60% of cover price. Whatever your views, they're here to stay, and have become essential to authors, especially for those whose books are unlikely to be widely available elsewhere. All publishers and service providers should put your book up on Amazon, including the very valuable *Look Inside* feature, as part of the deal. Amazon will also handle and reimburse all financial revenues towards your royalties, but due to the discounts they demand your profits will be very small. However, eBook authors have a much better deal, as covered by eBook producer, Andy Severn, in his previous interview.

Nevertheless, if you have self-published your books *without* a service provider, you can still sell your books on Amazon. They have two schemes of great value; *Amazon Advantage and Amazon Marketplace*, and all you need to have to be eligible is an ISBN, an Amazon account, and a bank account. I'm unable to reproduce the current terms and conditions offered for these sales options as they are very comprehensive, but all information is available by simply looking up Amazon Advantage and Amazon Marketplace online. It's quite alot to take in, but it's very necessary to have a comprehensive knowledge of how the systems work, and will ultimately work best for you.

Amazon Advantage

Here the independent author can set up a *personal* online mail order system for single copy sales. Basically Amazon Advantage agrees to stock copies, handle the finances, and send out the books in 'the normal way'. The advantage is that they reimburse the author directly *after deducting their cut*. I can't quote what the current rates are, and, as said, profit won't be very generous, but it's the best window on the world you're going to get, and has to be worth it.

Amazon Marketplace

Marketplace is also a great way of selling your new, excess, or old stock and there are different deals for mainstream and self-published. This valuable resource is unique to Amazon, and this is how it works. Every book they feature will have a 'new and used' box, and on clicking here you'll find a list (sometimes quite a long list) of traders offering books for sale, either new or used, with much more attractive prices than those offered by Amazon. Basic terms are thus:

Mainstream: Some mainstream copies offered as 'new' are actually bookshops who use Marketplace to shift surplus stock at a heavily discounted price. You may now ask, 'where do I get my cut', but you won't miss out. All new sales will be logged on your wholesalers sales ledger, and you'll receive your royalty in the normal way. After your book has been out for a while – sometimes a very short while – you'll begin to find 'used' copies are also offered, sometimes for as little as one penny, but these will not provide you with any further profit.

Self-Published: The deal with Marketplace is that they take direct payment from the buyer, inform you of a sale, and leave *you* with the responsibility of distribution. Thus, you'll have to factor in your price for postage and packing, but it could still be a sound deal. You may now wonder why Amazon bothers to go to all the trouble of operating this facility, but the answer is that they take a small service fee on every sale through a cut from the postage and packing charge. Multiplied by several thousands a day, it means a whopping great profit for them.

The 'More About The Author' Board

More About The Author, is found on the book's show page, and gives the author the space to write an interesting biography and put up a list of their books; an essential feature to effective marketing. To get ideas and examples look up a large selection of authors, study their pages, and then design your own to great advantage. This is a wonderful bit of free advertising and the opportunity shouldn't be wasted.

Alternative Publishing with Amazon

Amazon are tending to move towards producing their own methods of publishing – another hat that has been thrown into the ring of alternative publishing –but anything that can help an author with sales should not be dismissed. The next article is written by author C who wishes to remain anonymous, due to the terms of her recent contract, but she has written an extremely useful and interesting article about Amazon White Glove.

White Glove Publishing by Author C

The Amazon White Glove scheme is only offered to authors represented by literary agents. These agents' assist their authors to publish books, probably under an individual imprint, in eBook and paperback formats. White Glove offers additional benefits on the basis that these titles are good enough to have pushed past one publishing gatekeeper (the agent) and should thus be of a certain quality. Some of these White Glove benefits are similar to that of KDP Select. In return for exclusivity to Amazon, usually a year, comes the ability to participate in various promotions such as Countdown deals.

You might wonder what's really in it for an author. The real benefit of White Glove primarily comes down to an enhanced (though vaguely promised) push of the book, either during the first 30 or 90 days, and/or via inclusion in another special Amazon promotion (the summer sale, for instance). For authors, this is the most important part of the deal.

Although White Glove highlights the additional help it offers authors with formatting, etc, these are benefits that an author could in fact purchase at competitive prices or even carry out him/herself. It is not hard to learn to format an eBook and there are plenty of designers and typesetters (for the print version) who provide high quality work at a very reasonable cost, so don't be over-seduced by the formatting/uploading to the Amazon element of the promise. As well as the enhanced marketing push, which can elevate a book up the Amazon rankings, White Glove can also act as a talent alert to Amazon itself, and some White Glove authors have gone on to publish with one of the Amazon imprints, such as Thomas and Mercer.

For an author and agent who've undergone the depressing experience of pushing a book around the traditional publishers with nothing but a handful of rejections in return, White Glove can be very welcome news. In fact, some authors who've been offered contracts from traditional publishing houses may now be asking themselves if it is actually worth publishing with a traditional publisher who may not offer much marketing support, and will give them a digital royalty of just 20-30%, compared with the White Glove (effectively KDP) royalty of either 70% or 35%, depending on the price you wish to set. White Glove agents earn commission on sales at rates that may vary but are probably around 15%, so similar to what they earn on traditional deals.

The drawbacks? Although some writers may be relieved to have someone else handle the formatting and uploading side of producing eBooks and paperbacks, bear in mind that one of the benefits of self-publishing is that you have complete control, and are able to upload revised versions within minutes. Going through White Glove probably means going through your agent, who in turn will go through the White Glove design and formatting team. If you realise, on the morning of publication, that the wrong version of your eBook has been uploaded, and this happens to be a time when your agent is out of the office, you will wish that you could get into that Amazon KDP dashboard yourself and upload the correct version.

Another negative is that the print book in its Createspace (the Amazon printing arm) format may not be widely available to buy in bookshops, or loanable through libraries. Of course, authors can influence this state of affairs by persuading individual booksellers and librarians to stock a title. Just be aware that getting your book stocked nationally by, say, Waterstones, is not going to be as easy if you're offering a Createspace title. Regardless of

Createspace's claims, distribution in the UK of its books is not as good as it could be.

It's also worth saying that, no matter how well intentioned they are, and keen for their clients books to succeed, some agents may not entirely understand digital book production and eBook marketing. Nor will they necessarily have the resources to help with the various stages of taking a book live: proofreading, for instance. If you and your agent are considering White Glove it is worth sketching out a plan of who will do what during the publishing process and through the marketing life of the title. Factor in the costs of editing and a professional cover.

Don't assume that your agent will necessarily know more than you do about how to promote an eBook, or that White Glove will do it all for you. If you've been hanging around some of the excellent writers' **forums (Kboards, for** instance), or if you've already self-published an eBook, you could well know more about how to run an Amazon KDP Countdown promotion, for example, than your agent. Do your research and push that book hard yourself: get the Amazon reviews, do the giveaways, produce an enticing Amazon author page and website.

You may also wish to agree the payment schedule in advance. Some agents find it bureaucratically tiresome to have to account for multiple, sometimes small amounts of money trickling in on a monthly basis for their White Glove clients, as sales from each of the various Amazon stores (for example, the U.S., UK and Germany) and from Createspace are paid individually rather than in one lump sum. It may be reasonable to ask for quarterly remittances of royalties.

Amazon and eBooks

Most of the information concerning specific sales of eBooks on Amazon has been covered in the dedicated eBook section, but all eBook authors should pay very special attention to the section on *More About The Author Board* to ensure that both you and your publication are showcased very comprehensively.

Part Ten:

Marketing and Publicity: It's Time To Go Out and Hand Sell That Book

Chapter 15 : Up On Your Feet

Hand Selling

So far you've been sitting back in your armchair, learning about pre-publication rules, publishing options, the book industry, and the varying methods of creating a buzz about your book. Now it's time you left the comfort of your own home and went out into the public world of actually hand selling that book.

A Book Launch

You've all heard of the Grand Book Launch – a slick affair in a top London venue, financed by a large publishing house. The author, as guest of honour, is flattered and fussed over by the media. The bash is attended by celebrities and leading players of the literati, and good boozy time is had by all. The outstanding work-of-genius is guaranteed to be reviewed by all the relevant newspapers, magazines, and media arts programmes. It will appear as a window display in the chain bookshops, and be highly promoted inside.

This sort of launch only happens to very expensively marketed authors, media darlings, or newly talked-up sensations (very rare), but it doesn't mean that having your own is a waste of time. I'd say it's *essential* you do. Not just to set up your campaign, but to enjoy the psychological boost the experience gives you; the first-of-many joys of getting your book into print. It might seem like a party, but it's actually a very serious marketing and publicity exercise. You have the opportunity to sell books at full cover price (let's be honest, £8.99 is only the price of a bottle of wine and hardly a fortune), to whip up some enthusiasm, and get it talked up.

When you first start to write, your family, friends, and contacts you have outside of your literary circle, will sometimes disappoint you with their lack of interest. They infer, sometimes very kindly, that you're merely wasting your time with pie-in-the sky pretensions, and calling yourself 'a writer' is a little inflated. They have no idea how much effort is involved, how driven you are, and what grit and determination the procedure requires. All they know is that you're 'writing a book'; something that seems invisible, and the last thing on the agenda when exchanging news is, 'how's your writing going?' My own family actually consider my efforts to be some sort of 'occupational therapy' that takes up much more of my time than is justified, due to the financial returns being so poor. Actually, if you equate the time factor required, on a pro-rata basis with a paid employment, they're quite right. Although I've been a full-time writer for many years my *annual* income from writing has never exceeded my old *monthly* take-home cheque. A book launch is, therefore, a golden opportunity to show them the fruits of your labours, and be the star of the show for one night only. Go for it and really enjoy it, but don't be tempted to spend more than you can afford to lose in the hope that your sales will cover the costs. They may, but they may not, so unless you have set out to 'spoil yourself' it can be very demoralising to start your campaign with a huge monetary loss.

My Mainstream Book Launches

My launch for *The Crowded Bed* was quite an extravagant affair. The production of the book hadn't cost me a penny and I'd received a modest advance. The novel had taken me three years to write, and another three trying to sell it. It was a miracle I'd got it into print and I decided to really push the boat out, justifying the expense with an attitude of, 'Oh, what the hell – this may never happen again.' I was fortunate in two ways. My publisher, Transita, very kindly provided some high quality invitations and I was able to hold it in the splendour of The Randolph Gallery at the Ashmolean Museum in Oxford. My husband had worked at the museum for many years and, as a very special favour, I was allowed to use the venue. I funded the alcohol (bulk bargain buys of Pinot Grigio and Asti Spumante), the bar attendants, extra security staff, a professional photographer and a flashy 'notice me' outfit. Yes – the whole package was very expensive, but I treated it as an indulgence after many years of struggling to become a published author. I invited every single person I could think of: family, friends, my publishers, neighbours, work colleagues from over many years, my writing group, my reading group, my cinema group, tutors and fellow classmates from creative writing courses, local independent bookshop owners, and every other author I knew. In fact anyone for whom I had an email address, including my dentist and my optician! I also invited the managers of Waterstones and Borders (now closed) and although they didn't come they saw the up-market publicity. All invitees were encouraged to bring a partner and/or friends, and 130 plus turned up. From a financial point of view I was able to buy copies of the book from my publisher at 50% discount, and sold a hundred and fifty at full price. I thus broke even with the outlay, and it was a night to remember.

For my two most recent publications I scaled things down by hiring a (free) private room in a local up-market pub, with a lovely riverside setting. It was absolutely ideal as a bar was handy and there was plenty of parking space. All I had to pay was an agreed price for snacks.

My Self-Published Book Launches
With *The Sixpenny Debt and Other Oxford Stories,* the first of the OxPens anthologies, we had absolutely no budget. We had to choose a free venue and were

recommended *Far From The Madding Crowd*, an arts friendly pub in central Oxford. The manager was delighted to accommodate us as he knew the bar tills would be pinging, and they certainly were! We advertised the event with an open invitation pinned to the (several) fly poster notice boards of Oxford, invited everyone we ever knew, and I went on a BBC Radio Oxford morning show to do some PR. To say that there was standing room only was an understatement. The place was packed. Two famous local authors, Colin Dexter and Katy Fforde came along too, and both were kind enough to give very witty and entertaining speeches in our support. We then read very short sections of our own story, broken up by a couple of breaks to re-fill glasses. Our only expenses were a couple of tenners to buy drinks for our celebrity guests, and a few packets of balloons. For us, as a group, it was lovely to enjoy a shared social experience, as normally we just meet to discuss and dissect our work-in progress.

Pre-Planning Ideas

Before arranging anything, try to decide why you're holding a launch. If it's just to gather together your nearest and dearest it might be better suited to your own home. If it's to garner serious publicity a larger venue will be needed, together with the longest guest list you can produce, ensuring you include anyone of influence who can give your book a boost in any way.

The first detail of showmanship is the invitations. If your budget can stretch to it, and most especially if it's your first publication, professionally produced invitations from online firms such as Vistaprint or High Street print stores should suffice. If not, computer print-offs are the next best thing. Make sure you display the book cover, title and your name in large print, and include a short excerpt from your press release. I'd suggest you state a firm time slot, say 6.30pm-8.00pm, as it doesn't need to go on for too long.

It's very tiring for the author, both physically and mentally, and some people can seriously outstay their welcome. Also include an RSVP form, and your email address, as you'll need a ballpark figure for catering purposes. Either hand them out personally or send them out by snail mail post. Try to follow up your invitation with regular email 'sound bites' to keep their interest, and a reminder two or three days before the event will help attendance.

Always make sure you send an invitation to your county newspapers and local radio station, ensuring you include your PR. Even if they do promise to come, be prepared for disappointment. With *The Sixpenny Debt* we were promised a press photographer, so we all turned up early, with fixed grins, for a group shot. We waited . . . and waited . . . No show!

When trying to choose a venue there are many options. Some, such as village halls and community centres, just charge a flat fee, and the more corporate, like hotels, 'by the head'. Some may offer a 'free' deal, and allow you to bring your own wine, but beware of hidden charges. I was quoted a 'free' deal by an Oxford College, which would have been magical, but the corkage loading was the cost of the bottle, and I had to pay for more bar staff and waitresses I felt was warranted. In other words, it was outrageously expensive. If you don't want to pay for a swishy, impressive venue, an excellent alternative is your local independent bookshop. The 'indies', in fighting to survive against the might of supermarkets, chain stores, and online booksellers, are often delighted to host a local author night. However, although a small bookshop will be an excellent free venue, space may be restricted and better suited to book signing events.

Suggestions for a Successful Launch

Publicising and selling your book is the whole point of the exercise, so be as professional as possible. Display posters of the book cover (computer printouts will do) outside the venue, so any passers-by can see what's going on. With all my books a local print shop produced some A4 and A3 laminated posters, and although they were pricey I've been able to re-use them on many later occasions. Follow this through inside by putting up more posters on the walls, and possibly some fairy lights or balloons. In fact, anything to create a party atmosphere. A good idea is to ask a couple of friends with jovial personalities to act as front-of-house 'meeters and greeters', rather like ushers at a wedding. If you can't run to a professional photographer, prime some of the guests to take photos so you have a great collection to remind you of the night.

The drinks/refreshments table should *not* be the first thing inside the door otherwise the entrance will get completely clogged up. Display 'The Book' in high profile, centre stage on a table, so it draws the eye. Take more copies than you know you'll sell to make an impression, and ensure a few are propped up and facing forward. There is a marvellous product called a Single Pocket Cardboard Book Stand (www.stand-store.co.uk) which is ideal – something like the shape of an open shoebox – in white or black. For the odd one or two the p&p is quite high so it's more economical to order a higher number.

Thereafter it's essential to provide dedicated people to act as bookseller and money manager. My sister and a friend were very happy to take on this role, and it's wise to have two people in case one leaves the table. You'll also need a large bag of change, two sturdy containers – one for the change, and one for the revenue – plus a paperweight for the notes and cheques. With there being quite a bit of money involved, and security being a problem anywhere these days, you'll need to keep a close eye on things. A friend of mine, who was selling at a Roman Catholic Church fete, found that not only did all the money go, but a pile of books as well!

Another good idea is to sign a few copies beforehand for your guests to buy whilst you're busy socialising. A gesture of goodwill might be to offer a small discount on the cover price, say a pound, but, as said, most people who come know they'll be expected to buy a copy or two, at full price.

About half an hour after the official start time call the whole room to attention. It can be you, or even better, a dedicated 'Master/Mistress of Ceremonies' who can do a welcome speech, and provide a flattering talk-up about you and the book. For mainstream you might – just might – get a representative from your publishing house. Other choices might be someone who has travelled with you on your journey to publication, or an old friend who genuinely wants to tell the guests how impressed they are that you're now 'a published author'. Then you take over, and there's no need for a long-winded gush. On both occasions I was so excited I didn't trust myself to remember what I had to say, so I prepared a list of bullet points on a postcard, and referred to it.

Thank everyone for coming and say how lovely it is to see all of your friends and family under one roof. Make sure you mention the publisher or service provider for their lovely production, all the people and groups who have helped your writing career, and anyone who has been especially helpful or can be a source of future influence. Don't be tempted to put on an Oscar type performance. At this stage your book will have no reputation, and the time to crow will be when it's a proven winner. You could then read a short, appropriate passage from the book to whet the reader's appetite, and 300 words will be more than enough. Most of the guests will be much keener to chat and sip wine than concentrate on long passages, even though you're dying to unveil your wonderful prose. I recently went to hear a *very* famous author who'd just brought out his usual mega-selling novel. All he did was read, in a very dreary monotone, for nearly three quarters of an hour and I fell asleep. Seriously. *Zzzzzzzzzz.*

After you've read say that you hope everyone enjoys your book and ask, modestly, that if they *do* enjoy it you'd be very grateful if they could post a review on Amazon or The Book Depository. Thank everyone for coming again, and encourage the guests to have another drink, which they will, of course. Announce that you're now going over to the book table 'in case anyone would like a signed copy'. You now go and sit behind the table, with pen in hand (and a rictus smile).

After an initial flurry round the signing table, and lots more chatting, your guests will begin to drift off. Once everyone has gone you'll be totally exhausted, brain dead, and left with masses of packing and clearing up to do. But this is your one night of fame so prime some willing helpers to do this while you have your first drink of the night (I was always too busy to get one on the hoof). A launch is great, but I've always found that it's a bit like being at your own wedding – you're there, but you're so 'high' everyone else remembers much more than you do!

A Cautionary Tale

Flushed with the success of my Ashmolean Museum launch, I happily planned another high-octane event for my litho-produced self-published second novel, (now re-published by Thames River Press as *The Priest, His Lady, and The Drowned Child.)* Being on a much tighter budget this time, I hired a smaller but equally prestigious venue: a delightful mirrored dance studio above The Oxford

Playhouse Theatre. I also decided to economise by scrapping printed invitations and instead invited a hundred people by email only. I was disappointed to receive only sixty positive RSVPs, and thus funded the drinks and catering on sixty heads. On the night I was gutted as only twenty-two actually turned up! This could be a moral warning that 'second baby syndrome' *could* afflict a second novel. It could have been that I chose a bad time for a social event; a Sunday between 5pm and 7pm when many people are winding down their weekend. The most likely reason was that I invited guests by email only, and they didn't have something memorable to stick up on their mantelpieces. I only sold fifteen books, and it doesn't take a genius to work out that I found myself seriously out of pocket.

Chapter 16 : Bookshop Sales

Sales Pitches

Sales pitches in bookshops come in various guises, and these include a full-scale launch, a promotional talk, and a book 'signing'. Both the large High Street stores, or smaller independents, should be considered but before we examine what deals might be possible, I will go into the background and current economic climate of bookshops in general.

The Rise and Fall of Bookshops

Forty years ago my home town of Oxford had a fairly small WHSmith, where hardbacks and paperbacks fought for space alongside the usual stationary goods. Also, being a prestigious University city, we were lucky to have the truly brilliant Blackwell's; a large established family bookshop that catered for the academic side of the University, and offered several floors of fiction and non-fiction. This was a rare luxury, and whilst others towns might have had a WHS, there would be one or two excellent independents as well.

Then, in response to the boom times of economic growth, from the nineteen-eighties onward, competition in the form of large chain stores arrived. Oxford was blessed with an enormous Waterstones, an even larger Borders, and a branch of The Works (a remainder shop). This pattern was reflected nationwide, including two other chains, Dillons and Ottakars, all of whom pushed hard for space in the smaller market towns, ousting many independents that couldn't compete. They all catered to mass-market tastes, their stock was controlled from their head offices, and each branch, in each town, seemed to be a cloned twin. Behind the scenes, of course, competition drove the pace, and publishers paid large fees for the privilege of high-profile displays. Figures I've heard for those days were thousands for a major window display at Christmas, ditto for a 'three-for-two' deal, and even a large fee for the book to be 'outward facing'. These times were the salad days of book selling, and there was no such thing as online discounting, or self-published authors. In fact, in those balmy years of economic growth, the only outlet for the self-publisher was the sneered at 'vanity publishing'.

Ah, but how the mighty are fallen, and there came three things; the advent of Amazon and other online selling facilities, the economic downturn, and the end of the Net Book Agreement. The NBA, which had operated since 1900, meant that all booksellers agreed to books having a uniform retail price, but in 1997 it ended. This meant a 'free-for-all' in undercutting sprang up by online retailers and supermarkets who were able to negotiate rock bottom prices. Gradually, although battling to survive, Borders went to the wall, Dillons and Ottakars were absorbed into Waterstones, and Waterstones (apart from WHSmith) are now the only survivor. In what is still a fragile market, they are now doing all they can to 'thrive and survive', and have introduced a revolutionary new policy change in giving branch managers much more autonomy in running their own unique, local store. Effectively, this means they're given the opportunity to introduce more vibrancy and excitement, and buy in what they think their local customers will want to read. My own branch in Oxford certainly welcomes approaches from enthusiastic authors, and hosts many lively events to draw people in. It seems that these innovations are working as James Daunt, the chief executive of Waterstones, has recently stated that the 'tide is turning'. Three new stores opened in 2014 and they are experiencing a 'modest growth'. This must give authors hope that the major bookshops are going to survive the alternative onslaughts.

Independent Bookshops

Three rousing cheers for independent bookshops. In these days of cut-throat commercialism, it's wonderful that 'The Indies' are fighting their corner in a very tough world. Their problems are manifold. In most towns they have to compete with WHSmith and/or a Waterstones, the might of Amazon et al, and the growth of eBooks. The great thing about them is that they're accessible, and individual, and as much as they need us, we need them too. The astute independent owner will have boundless dynamism in promoting, not only their diverse and interesting stock, but by supporting local authors, setting up reading groups for adults and children, providing specialist guest speakers, and putting on other fun events of interest to all age groups. Those that don't demonstrate energy and risk are largely finding that their businesses are becoming unviable, and over the past five years the percentage of closures has been heart-breakingly high.

Can I take this opportunity to ask that you fully support your local independent bookshop and ensure we all do our bit to make sure we keep them, not only open, but thriving.

Bookshops Nationwide

Whilst it's always a good idea to make yourself personally known to bookshops in your area, you should also approach those outside your locality. The most useful website I can find for information is: www.localbookshops.co.uk. This site is very graphic and user friendly, and provides a breakdown of the UK into specified geographical sections. One can then source a list within a chosen area, together with addresses, phone numbers, and email addresses. Email contact must be the best way, as snail mail is likely to be cost prohibitive. Write a friendly personal letter, with a pasted selection of your reviews, attach all your usual publicity materials, and maybe suggest that your book would make a good reading group choice. In the past, one 'tsunami' I sent out brought forth some excellent results! Within a week my 'in stock' figure listed on Gardners went down from 38 to 0, and I had a couple of offers to attend author talk sessions.

Sometimes an Indie can even 'make' a book a bestseller. Crockett and Powell in London championed a book entitled *What Was Lost* by Catherine O'Flynn, published in 2007 by the tiny Tindal Press. By giving the book publicity and support on their blogsite, the quality of *What Was Lost* was brought to the attention of both the general public and media. Whilst not initially being a best seller it was consequently shortlisted for every major prize going, including being longlisted for The Man Booker Prize, and actually winning The Costa First Novel Award. Needless to say it *did* become a best seller.

Sales Events in All Bookshops

All bookshops, whether corporate or independently owned, are interested in one thing, and one thing only – making sales – and any suggestions from an active author, including the motivated self-published, should be listened to very favourably. Most managers and owners are happy to host in-store events as it often attracts more customers, it provides a buzz about the shop, and they usually sell more books than normal (both yours and other stock). Holding any event in bookshops involves the question of how stocks will be provided, and an agreement on sales revenues. The following options will apply.

1) The bookshop will buy in your books from a wholesaler through their own unique ordering system. All sales will go through the tills, and your royalties attributed to you 'through the system'. If your wholesaler is not one they use (they do tend to do business with their

152

favourites) it probably means that deal 2 will apply.

2) You will buy your own books (at your favoured discount) and either bring them with you to the shop or pay for delivery from your wholesaler. Although each sale will have to go through the tills, you will have reached a prior agreement as to exactly what your cut on each sale will be, after they have taken their profit.

A Bookshop Launch

Securing a launch at a High Street chain is a great coup and I've never heard of any who charge. However, as they are best held in the evening, and the working day will have to be extended, the manager must be convinced it'll be financially viable for them; that you'll attract a large crowd, and subsequently shift alot of copies. The same economic considerations apply even more so to the 'Indies' who really *have* to trade at a profit. At both venues you will usually be given a strict exit deadline as none of them will want it to go on too long, or involve alot of clearing up.

A Book Signing

With a book signing you'll be there to sell and sign copies for casual purchasers. All the shop has to do is provide you with a chair and a table, and the rest is up to you. Always make *absolutely sure* you liaise with the management beforehand on what the procedure will be, what you should expect from each other, and how payments will be made. It's damn hard work and you shouldn't be out of pocket. One self-published author friend took her own stock to her local Waterstones, sold a thrilling forty books, and discovered she actually lost a pound on each copy – i.e. she was forty pounds down, plus her petrol and parking costs.

Timing of the event should also be considered. Saturday morning is a good time (a greater footfall), but other times, such as late night opening, can be just as good. Usually the shop will be happy to advertise the event a couple of weeks in advance, but that won't be enough to get it noticed. How about a flyer placed at strategic pick-up points? Tell your local papers, get the word out to everyone you know, get a poster made up and put it into as many shop windows as you can. Create that buzz!

If you've been given a morning slot be sure to get there early as the shop is likely to be relatively empty. You'll then be ready, relaxed, and smiling, when the shop starts to fill up; there's nothing worse than being pounced upon by eager shoppers when you're trying to gather breath and organise yourself. You'll probably find you've been allocated a table in a reasonably good position, and then it's up to you. One experienced author told me that sitting behind the desk, with his books stacked in piles, actually created a barrier between him and potential customers, so he got up and joined in. I found the opposite. By moving around on my feet I disappeared into a member of staff. My books table became unattended and I ended up recommending endless books by other authors. I guess you must work out your own strategy, but always wear a badge, big enough for people to read, ensuring that you state *Jack Jones - Author.*

Authors who do best at signings are those who can easily engage people in conversation – not exactly giving the hard sell approach, but by being informing and interesting about both their book and themselves. And you also need the proverbial thick skin! If someone (and there always *is* someone) who has taken up a great deal of your time and energy decides not to buy a copy don't take it personally or get cross. Just move on to the next prospect! Signings can be great fun if you enjoy talking to people, and can be a really rewarding part of the marketing process, but (as ever) be prepared for failure. Some customers clearly find it all a bit intimidating, deny eye contact, and scurry off pronto.

No matter who you talk to, or how time-consuming they are, smile and *be nice*. Booksellers talk to one another and if you create a reputation for being dreary or snooty you'll soon get a reputation. Provide free bookmarks, or similar, and try handing a book to each potential customer for them to look at. I'm told that if it touches someone's hands they're far more likely to buy it, but if they give it straight back (as if it's red hot) talk to them about what they like reading and (reluctantly!) recommend something else in the shop – a good ploy to please the hosting shop.

Another factor is the weather. However much planning you do, and however good you may be at approaching prospective customers, nothing can overcome the vagaries of the British weather. If it's a miserable, cold, wet afternoon then prepare to be underwhelmed! I did one in a Waterstones ten days before Christmas, the shop door was wide open, and I was in a cold and draughty spot. The shop was packed with frazzled shoppers, desperately looking for last-minute Christmas presents, and weren't the slightest bit interested in the unknown frozen lady.

A Promotional Talk

These are the events I most enjoy as you're there to talk-up your book to a captive audience, and hopefully make some sales. If you've prepared your talk well you'll have a marvellous opportunity to enhance the issues and themes of its content (without revealing any spoilers to 'the end'), skilfully weave in some enticing features of your characters, and provide some tantalizing cliffhangers. I will mention here that we all have very differing target audiences and you need to know what yours is. As I always deal with fairly emotive issues, set in both the post-war past and the present, my own would be mature, widely read, and looking for a 'thumping good read'. Each of you will have to put a great deal of thought into this, as there are so many categories to slot into. Even in the children and Young Adult market there are varying age ranges and abilities involved so it's best, when setting up the publicity for a promo talk, to make sure you attract the right sort of reader by advertising its genre or type.

n.b. I've never heard of anyone doing an event in WHSmith, as they tend to be run by 'head office' and books are only one part of their merchandise.

Sale or Return (SoR)

Before we leave bookshops I'd like to cover the annoying anomaly of Sale or Return. As with all businesses there's always an element of risk, and book industry retailers are able to lessen it by making the publisher share it. Unsold stock can be returned to the wholesaler for a full refund, and this can be up to nine months after they were initially ordered. It's an infuriating practice. What other branch of commercial enterprise can do this? If M&S or Wilkinsons are left with stock on their hands they offer them as sale items, but bookshops can demand reimbursement. This is why an author's royalty payment can sometimes be a year in arrears so the returns can be deducted. The returned books will, hopefully, be resold, but if they're less than pristine they won't be. They will be sent to a 'remainder' shop such as The Works, or be pulped. The only up side of SoR is that unknown authors would find it even harder to get their work into bookshops if it didn't exist. My suggestion is that there should be a 'Sale Bin' in every store to shift stock on a break-even basis. Wouldn't it save everyone a great deal of work and do lesser-known authors a favour?

Chapter 17 : The Library Service

How Lucky We Are

My youngest son spent the whole of his childhood 'in the saddle', and when he came home, caked in mud and manure, he would put his gloves to his nose, inhale like a little Hannibal Lecter, and make a face as if he were smelling gardenias. Every time I go into a library I feel like that. You stand, inhaling deeply, as the wonderful aroma of books hits your senses.

In the past we've tended to take public libraries for granted. They are just 'there', like pubs and garages, fire stations and hospitals. Some of us are signed-up life-serving members, and some of us aren't. I'm ashamed to admit, that before publication, I'd never realised what influence and power our national library services have in getting our books 'out there'. Therefore, do consider the library service as a leading factor in your marketing and publicity campaign. Whilst being publically funded they are not there to assist you commercially, but are usually happy to embrace you as an author.

Sadly, as everywhere, there's been a major upheaval within the service due to 'the cuts'. A huge number of branch libraries have closed, the remaining ones are fighting for survival, and even the major ones have to manage with less staff and reduced opening times. Please can I say here that if you want your library to remain 'as per' try to find out how you can help in any way. Apart from the rank and file it's essential that children and the elderly are still offered this facility; the child as an educational tool, and the older person as a contact point and enhancer of life. My small village branch was threatened with complete closure two years ago, but due to forming a 'friends' association the fight was listened to.

Although we now have to manage with reduced opening hours, many fund-raising activities are organised to help fund the Librarian, and a rota of volunteers is ensuring that we can continue a good service. My contribution is to arrange a monthly coffee morning with a guest speaker, ensuring that we fly the flag for the continuing interest in reading and literature in general.

In writing the following article I've been helped enormously by Lynne Moores, Chief Librarian at my nearest large library in Abingdon. Thank you Lynne, for all your help, and everything you do to support local authors.

There are two aspects of the library services network that all authors need to know about. The administrative side of things might be considered a bit dull, but it's essential information in understanding how libraries function behind the scenes. The joyful part is the outstanding public service we still have in this country, both as readers and authors, and how lucky we are that they exist as they do.

I will talk about the admin side first, but please don't skip it or you'll miss some vital information. All local authorities in the United Kingdom and Northern Ireland have a library network, depending on the type and size of authority, i.e. County, London Borough, or Unitary (which means a collection of units). There will usually be, in addition to the libraries' headquarters and main central branch, a network of branches in varying sizes and (if you're lucky) far-flung outposts will have a weekly 'mobile'. It sounds complicated, but in simple terms this means that each authority uniquely manages its own service. This is a really good thing. If they were wholly managed by central government you can imagine what bureaucracy would be involved, and the standard of services available would, inevitably, be diminished.

However, all authorities receive funding from central government, and this is based upon the number of residents in the receiving authority. The rest of the funding comes from local revenue, and this is decided when county spending budgets are allocated. This allocation is used to fund the expenses of running the whole of the library service, including the buying of books, staff salaries, transport costs and buildings maintenance. Therefore, one must conclude, some areas are better funded, managed, and provided for, than others.

How Stock Is Selected

All library services, in selecting which books they buy, get their information from specialists library supplier catalogues such as Askews/Holt Jackson (now owned by Gardners) and BDS. These catalogues are not available to view by the general public, but each month pre-publication details of hundreds of books are listed, and the stock selection panels have the difficult job of deciding what to buy. Mainstream authors should be represented by their publishers, but if you're self-published always check with your service provider if your book will be included in these catalogues. If not, you can do it yourself by submitting all your publishing details, *as far in advance as possible*, to BDS who run the British Library Cataloguing-in-Publication scheme. (www.bibliographicdata.co.uk*)*

Here is a copy of the email I sent to them to confirm this:

Dear Sirs

I am a mainstream published novelist, Mary Cavanagh. I have just completed the second edition of my 2009 self-help book, now entitled Calling All Authors. *This book is written for all authors; published, self-published and not yet published. The categories covered are manuscript presentation, trying to get a mainstream contract, literary agents, self-publishing including eBooks, behind the scenes of the book industry, and of course, marketing and publicity.*

I would like to confirm to my readers how they are able to ensure that their self-published books are included in the BDS catalogue.

With very best wishes
Mary Cavanagh

This is the reply I received.

Dear Mary

Thank you for your e-mail. In order for us to create a catalogue record for books to send to libraries and library suppliers, all one needs to do is complete our online registration form. The form can be found on our website www.bibligraphicdata.co.uk *and by clicking on 'Upload Your Data' on the home page. Either the author or the publisher can do this.*

Bibliographic Data Services

www.bibliographicdata.co.uk

Getting Stocks into Libraries

The next stage is to contact libraries to request that they might like to purchase your book. All library authorities have a chief executive and several highly qualified librarians who help to select the books, both fiction and non-fiction, for the enjoyment of the public.

My advice is to start locally. I was lucky that my central library decided to stock several copies of my first novel, *The Crowded Bed*, and a smaller branch chose it as their reading group's book-of-the-month. So now you're saying, 'That's fine for you. Transita, as a mainstream publisher, obviously had good PR and was able to get your book noticed'. Yes – this is true – but if you're not being represented it's up to you to approach libraries yourself, talk up your book and really start being your own marketing manager. No matter what category you fall into, mainstream or self-published, researching your library authority is paramount and your central library can give you a contact name of the chief stock selector. They'll also need to know ordering details (and that can include yourself) as their tight budgets will demand the incentive of discounts to place orders.

Casting The Net Nationwide

Until to a few months ago there existed a wonderful website detailing all UK Public Libraries compiled by Sheila and Robert Harden. (http://dspace.dial.pipex.com/town/square/ac940/weblibs.html). Sadly, this has been removed, but I've left the web details in, just in case it miraculously re-appears after updating. I spent alot of time searching online for something as comprehensive, but could find nothing, so the only thing to do (and I did this with my latest novel, *Who Was Angela Zendalic*) is to slog through a county-by-county trawl to locate the central library of all major towns and ask for the name of their library stock buyer. This exercise was very time-consuming and frustrating but it was the only thing left. But it paid off. I received quite a few positive replies, leading to orders that I wouldn't have had if I hadn't bothered. One miserable fact I picked up was that one authority informed me that they never stock print-on-demand books – a real body blow to self-publishing and the smaller mainstream presses.

If the library orders from their advance catalogues the books are usually in stock by given publication dates, which is why you can always get the 'new' work by a favourite author soon after it comes out. Otherwise, books ordered from a 'standing start' usually take a long time to arrive – on average about ten weeks – but a way of checking current stock is to look up their online website and search for your book. With my first novel – in the good old days of cash flow – I was surprised to find my book was indeed stocked nationwide, but the uptake was very uneven, undoubtedly due to the individual taste of the purchasing librarians, and the funds at their disposal. I found that, for instance, Northern Ireland had 53 copies in stock and Cardiff had 36. Manchester and Milton Keynes had only 2 apiece, and Reading and Birmingham had none at all. The bottom line, however, was that after looking at all the authorities on the list I discovered that hundreds of copies were in stock nationwide, giving me a potential readership of thousands. 'So what?' you might think. Those copies have been bought only once, get circulated and don't generate sales. The truth is exactly the opposite. Remember that word-of-mouth, more than any other medium, generates sales. If a library reader has enjoyed a book he/she will talk it up to their friends, family and colleagues, and although many dedicated library users will wait patiently in a queue for a recommended book, a fair few will buy it.

Public Lending Rights (PLR)

How many first-time authors know about PLR? Before I was published I'd heard the term PLR talked about in a casual way, by my writing group and some authors I knew. I took no notice thinking it was something rather obscure that had nothing to do with me. I soon discovered that I had to register myself with the service *urgently* as potential payment was involved!

The very excellent website of the PLR (www.plr.uk.com) explains how to register yourself and your book(s), and how the payments are calculated. I will not go into copious detail, but in basic terms PLR is a small fee, (currently 6.20p) paid to authors every time a book is borrowed from a 'Sample Library'. The recording of *every* borrowing in the country would be an enormous administrative headache, so they have simplified this by compiling a list of 'Sample Libraries'. This means that about forty public library authorities are chosen as 'participating', and the actual branches used to compile the data will probably be well over a thousand! The samples changes every year, so you can look ahead on the PLR website. Each loan is recorded, and the data regularly sent to the PLR office. Your payment is then calculated on what your *average* borrowing would be, nationwide. It might seem a complicated process, but the PLR office manages it brilliantly.

However, the rewards can be a bit of a lottery. For example. Being an Oxford author I tend to have quite a few borrowings in Oxfordshire. Oxfordshire was a 'Sample Library' for 2006-2007 and 2007-2008, and my PLR payments reflected this. However, since then Oxfordshire has not been on the sample list so I've received a very reduced amount. I think the best advice I can give is just to try and get your book into libraries, register your book with PLR, and treat any payments as a lucky bonus.

Part Eleven:

Publicity and Marketing
What Else Can You Do?

Chapter 18 : A Round-Up of Other Ideas

Direct Selling to Target Audiences

What groups or organisations might be interested in reading your book? If you are a non-fiction writer Google your local area with key words concerning your topic. Fiction writers should target any group that might enjoy a talk from you. First think about the age range of your target audience. A national organisation, The Meet-Up's (www.meetup.com/cities/gb) are a good bet for the twenties to the forties, plus other singles groups who arrange social events. In the past I've approached The Society of Young Publishers, and subsequently got a fabulous whole page review in an upmarket county magazine. If you're more mature try any local groups or associations, such as The Women's Institute or Age Concern, and many towns have a thriving University of The Third Age (U3A) which caters for older, leisured folk looking for cultural pursuits. If your book is genre-specific seek out any appropriate group with a lively offer, and if you write for children or young adults think of organisations such as schools, parents associations, youth clubs, after school clubs, or anywhere else the young gather in their leisure time.

In the following article children's author John Kitchen has written on his experiences of direct selling in schools.

Marketing Through Schools by John Kitchen

'As a children's author I find that schools are my major outlet, but my own instinct is not to be seen to exploit this market by merely promoting my books. I offer workshops where I use my experience as a writer to enthuse children to be writers and readers. These workshops are set out on my website: johnkitchenauthor.com. Mainly I show children how I set about writing, and how I approach the various challenges of being a good quality storyteller. I take various artefacts, showing the story of a book from the first idea to the published book. As a children's author it is a good idea to save all these things to use in schools.

I have used various ways of contacting schools, from adverts in local papers through to personal visits, flyers and personalised letters to head teachers. I found that advertisements were of little or no use – expensive and yielding negligible results – so I designed flyers using 'Vistaprint' and distributed these to schools in various ways. Some authorities will distribute them using the 'school post', but with cuts, and a need to reduce the volume of school mail, less are now offering this service. This means I have to use the GPO to distribute the flyers, so I send them with a personalised letter to the head teachers of each school. You can usually get full lists of authorities' schools and the names of their head teachers by Googling the authority.

Writing to every school is a very time-consuming exercise, as well as being costly, but only a few well-known authors will have no need to invest in publicising their own books. It also requires investing time and burning a lot of shoe leather, to say nothing of the rubber on your car tyres!

Even with all this effort the take-up can be disappointing. Last summer I wrote about three hundred letters to heads of schools in Gloucestershire and, so far I have been invited into about ten schools. Also, the response and sale of books will vary hugely dependent on the interest and internal organisation of the school. At worst the school sees you as someone to entertain the classes, leaving the teacher free to pursue extra-curricular activities while you are left with a classroom assistant. Usually, in this type of school, no one has bothered to broadcast your visit and no-one bothers to follow it up, so neither children nor parents are prepared in any way. This can be very demoralising with 'no sales' of books, and a feeling that your visit was of no worth.

On the other hand, the schools that see your visit as a valuable educational resource are the ones who plan the visit with you, prepare the children, inform the parents, and make an 'occasion' of the visit. This can generate a very satisfying and rewarding experience, and I recently visited an Academy near Gloucester where I spent two days. The literacy co-ordinator planned my timetable with the staff, chose the workshops they wanted for each class and which of my books they wanted me to use for each workshop. They also advertised my event, the teachers used my workshop as a platform for further work, and some read my books to the children after my visit. The results were amazing. The children were enthusiastic and greatly motivated, and at the end of each day queues for signed copies stretched beyond the classroom door. I sold out of books and had to go back for an extra signing session. In that one school I sold over a hundred books and, more importantly, gained a large enthusiastic readership, some of whom were newly stimulated to become readers, when, previously, reading fiction had no interest for them at all.

Points I would suggest to writers of children's books are: have a good and stimulating website, be prepared to invest a huge amount of time contacting schools, print attractive flyers and posters advertising your visit, stating what you will be doing and the titles on sale, plus their cost. Distribute these to schools in advance of your visit, but not too soon as schools are very busy places and things can get lost. If possible, liaise with the literacy co-ordinator at the school and be careful to match your presentation to the age/ability of the children. Make sure your presentation is stimulating and worthwhile, and well prepared. Be careful to work within a timeframe – usually a one hour session per class – giving children plenty of space to ask questions and, possibly, engage in some activity. Try to make sure your visit is well publicised, take plenty of books with you and a float. Ideally take a friend or else be prepared to deal with the finances as well as signing books and chatting to your new readers. Finally hope for the best, but be prepared for the worst'.

Reading Groups – The Upside and the Downside

The chances are that you belong to a reading group and whilst they largely focus on fiction, they often include non-fiction topics, such as biographies, memoirs, lively travel books, and amusing observations. Thus, any author who thinks their book might fit the reading group criteria should be encouraged to approach a group and try to get it taken up.

When *The Crowded Bed* was first published I belonged to a large, lively reading group and suggested that they select it as a chosen read. I was more than a bit miffed to be told, quite bluntly, that the answer was 'no', due to them feeling too intimidated to view it objectively. I was disappointed at the time, but came to realise that this is actually a fair comment. I know from experience, having read books by friends, there are some I love, and some – well – I don't love at all. It's far better for your group not to do it than put you through a disappointing, but honest, response. You'll most likely find that the individual members read it out of curiosity anyway. If they've liked it they'll tell you, and if they haven't they will hopefully be too kind to pass judgement! If a group agrees to take it on always remember to ask that they give reviews (and only good reviews, please) to both Amazon and *NewBooksMag*.

Most bookshops, (both chain and independent) are likely to run reading groups, and in the past the Blackwell's Bookshop Reading Group in Oxford has won a very prestigious Guardian Award as the best reading group. My local Indie, Mostly Books in Abingdon runs several: two evening groups (with waiting lists), a daytime group, and a 'bring-a-baby' group which is very popular for obvious reasons. Also, they run a regular story time for under fives, a Young Adults group, and an after-school reading club. Any child-orientated events like these should be of great interest to children's writers.

Outside of bookshops and library groups there are also the privately arranged community reading groups. These exist in their thousands, but they're often 'closed shops', run as such, don't advertise themselves, and are very difficult to find. I even heard about two in my own village recently that I (the publicity and marketing maniac) hadn't routed out!

In researching for *Calling All Authors* I trawled for 'Reading Group Information' on the Internet, and although I found some accessible websites, I discovered that they don't publish group contact details any more – doubtless because they've been over-targeted by so many hopeful authors. Well worth a try, though, is www.readinggroups.org as they list groups geographically, and although most of them are within libraries there are a few independents. Also try the Meet-Ups, as most large towns run at least one reading group.

If you contact any group the usual approach will include the usual; your press release, any reviews, and a short piece dedicated to why your book will make a good choice. Offer to send a complimentary copy to the organiser as a gesture of goodwill, and a great thing to include will be any positive comments from other groups who've already featured your book. Realistically you'll be in competition with the new and popular publications of the day, so the only thing (as ever) is to make a sensational presentation, and keep your fingers crossed.

Sometimes, when a group has read your book, it's part of 'the deal' that you meet them for a *post mortem* discussion. Some of them will be delighted to have a 'real author' in their presence, and it can be a most enjoyable and useful way of getting you and your work talked up. However, there may be a downside. Some venues will involve long journeys (and petrol costs) to unfamiliar places, mostly at night, which might cause anxiety. Also, being an author 'on-the-spot' can be a mixed blessing. The group may have had many years of bonding, and one of their major features will be social contact, often involving food and drink. I've done a couple where so much eating and chattering took place, I was largely ignored. People arrived late, with great disruption, and it was a quite useless exercise. At one it was made very clear to me, after some very scrappy discussion, that the feast was ready to be served, and it was time for me to leave! Another group were so critical and rude to me the organiser rang up the next morning and apologised for their bad behaviour. If you do agree to attend remember that you (the author, no less!) are doing them a great favour by turning out, so don't let them treat you like some sort of cowering servant. Be completely up front with your needs, demand respect, and lay down some ground rules. That you do not wish to 'break bread' with them, that late comers are a nuisance, and you'll require travelling expenses (say 30p a mile). As 'an unknown' it might seem that you're shooting yourself in the foot by being demanding, but if you don't the whole thing could end up as an infuriating shambles and your blood pressure will soar.

Even if your book has been a great hit, and enjoyed by most, you'll often get some awkward negative questions to deal with from the statutory sadistic know-all. Thus, you must be prepared to stand your corner, and defend your characters and storyline. When this has happened, instead of conceding to them, I've gently suggested that reading should be an experience far removed from the confines of one's own individual life experiences, and defend my cast by explaining that they merely mess up their lives and behave like so many people do – badly!

Library Reading Groups

I've found that all library groups are certainly worthwhile and enjoyable. They're lively, well attended, well organised, finding them is easy (being well sited) and there's usually dedicated parking. Always, be very grateful for any activities involving the library service due to them having to fund overtime payments and keep the building open after hours. You won't make direct sales, but your book, and your name as the author, will be remembered when you bring out another book.

Radio Broadcasting Slots

Local radio can be a very successful medium for generating interest. My own local radio station, BBC Oxford, is really supportive and welcomes people in to interview. When you think about it, it's quite a job to fill all-day-every-day airtime with more than music and news bulletins, so yours might be more than willing. Before making contact with a radio station listen to a selection of their programmes, to ensure they still do 'arts interviews', and which would be best suited to your book. It's most often the mid-afternoon shows that are likely to offer you a slot. You can apply, either by sending a review copy, and all the usual marketing paperwork, to the presenter or producer at their station headquarters, or phone the editorial office and offer yourself. Usually you'll be asked to go to the studios to 'go live', but they might also suggest a telephone interview, a pre-recorded interview, or even send out the radio car. It really depends on what sort of budget they have, and the style of the piece they want to produce.

In a live interview you have to be prepared to answer questions, and answer them well, and the conduct of the interview is largely down to the presenter's preference. Some like to speak to potential guests first, to get a sense of how they come across, and others trust their production team to book an interesting guest. I think it's fair to ask *exactly* what the first question is going to be, and thereon, after your rehearsed answer, a skilful interviewer should then lead you off into a balanced question and answer session. On my first broadcast I nearly dried up. I was shown into the studio with no rehearsal, and the interviewer just launched me into it, with no pre-plan. '*Right, Mary. What's* The Crowded Bed *all about?*' The worst question you can ever be asked. Scary or what! So, make absolutely sure your first question and answer is well prepared and rehearsed.

Unfortunately, local radio doesn't have the relaxed feel of BBC Radio Four, and whilst talking to you the presenter will often be cuing up music, looking online, and preparing for other parts of the show. Don't get distracted if they ask you a question and then don't seem to be listening to your reply; they are – but in a practiced professional way. If you're lucky there might be some breaks for a piece of music between questions, giving you time for a breather and an off-sound chat. Live interviews can be great fun, but it's easy to concentrate on merely answering the questions in an articulate way. Try to mention purchasing details such as how/where people can buy the book and if you have any events lined up, together with an occasional repeat of the title. A good idea, on winding up the interview (pre-discussed with the radio station), is to offer a signed copy of your book as a 'phone-in' prize for answering a question from yourself. My favourites are, '*In the novel* Rebecca, *what is the Christian name of the second Mrs De Winter?'* and *'What was Mr Darcy's Christian name'.*

If your 'story' is especially topical or newsworthy, and you want to aim really high, you could approach the editors of the many book related shows on BBC national radio. Here you need to be *very* familiar with the types of show and the presenters before suggesting yourself, and you need to be *really* confident you can interview well!

Making a Personal Video

With the advent of YouTube it's now possible to get your own promotional video put up online. A few years ago video marketing was a very expensive procedure, and something of a huge coup. Now, anyone who has an iPhone, or instant video recording facility, can do it – in my case with the help of a friend! Try to make it as professional as possible by rehearsing, and rehearsing, and only put it up if it's a skilled and accurate account of you and your book. Make yourself appear lively and interesting, but don't push your own stardom over the quality of your book. And don't make it too long – a minute is actually a long time! You won't be surprised to hear that there are companies who have taken up 'YouTube publicity' for authors, with great claims of distribution, but I am wary of anyone who wants money . . .

Literary Festivals

I'm a little ambivalent about mentioning Literary Festivals as I've actually had very limited success with them. This is probably because both large and small festivals are arranged a year ahead, and most are looking for big names from big publishers. It's understandable. Festivals are expensive to administer, and due to the dire lack of marketing and publicity offered to *anyone* these days, the big names are becoming only too pleased to take part. The largest ones, such as Hay-on-Wye, Cheltenham, Edinburgh and Oxford are run by the broadsheets, and the speakers are contracted strictly by invitation. Mostly the list is made up of media names from all platforms, and only include lesser-known authors if they've currently hit the headlines. If the smaller festivals want to compete they must cover the finances (the big hitters rarely do anything for free), and recruit an army of voluntary staff.

One aspect about Literary Festivals, that might offer some degree of hope, is that they're rapidly springing up all over the place, in large and small towns, and naturally, the best ones to try would be the ones most local to you. Finding them in time to be included is always difficult, but a useful point of advance enquiry might be your local bookshops, both chain and independent. Also, you could try your library, the Tourist Information Office, or the editorial department of your county newspaper. Your city or county council may also have an Arts Officer to approach, and if you look up Literary Festivals online, many will appear. A useful site is www.britishcouncil.org/arts-literature-literaryfestivals. As soon as you have a publication date look ahead, as some may be running workshops or alternative sideshow events you can be involved in, or perhaps suggest your own involvement.

Online Reading Activity Sites – *Lovereading* and *Lovewriting*

There are many reader activity sites that are dedicated to books and reading, and encourage interactivity. Lovereading (www.lovereading.co.uk) is strictly for mainstream works. It has established itself as a community of over 150,000 avid readers who sign up to receive information about the latest books, published in their favourite genres. The site is used by publishers to promote their books, but if your publisher chooses not to pay, or your book isn't stocked with Gardners, the wholesaler (mine currently aren't), your book won't be put forward.

For the self-published there's a similar set-up, (www.lovewriting.co.uk) and is specifically dedicated to encourage and promote self-publishing. It's open to anyone to submit a book but a significant fee is required to register. I'm not sure how the featured books are chosen so I think my advice would be to ask your service provider if they have any insider knowledge, or previous success in this field.

Local Superstores

Miracles do happen and it's got to be worth a try. With my first novel I enquired, very modestly, at my local Waitrose store what were the chances of them stocking 'a well reviewed book by a local author'? It was good news to discover that Waitrose section managers can actually have some input in choosing titles, although they have to be strictly approved of by their head office. I sent in a very comprehensive application pack, together with my best reviews, a recent interview from *The Oxford Times*, and three complimentary copies. A month later it appeared on the shelves of their three largest county stores, and sold very well – so well that it was regularly ordered in for six months with no prompting from me. My second was also granted inclusion. This type of promotion is very unusual, as all the other big supermarkets will only bulk-buy celebrity books, and popular fiction, at vast discounts.

Networking With The Like-Minded

Having a genre is a huge advantage. Join any group or society you know of that can help you network, both locally and nationally. Google *'Writers' Associations UK'* to try and find something appropriate for you, and then move to worldwide support groups, especially in the U.S. Joining a genre writers' group is a fantastic networking resource, and can offer great support for your writing, but your sales might not be boosted (previously mentioned) as other writers don't always make the best book buyers! Two of them are listed below.

The Crime Writers Association (www.thecwa.co.uk) and *Author Network* (www.authornetwork.com/crime.html) are specifically for crime, but self-published authors should check if they're eligible for membership.

The Romantic Novelists Association (www.rna-uk.org) is brilliant. Each area of the country has a geographical group (a 'chapter') that provides regular meet-ups, i.e. lovely pub lunches and useful literary natter. On a national level they have some very well-organised and well-attended social events, and it's all terrific fun. Strictly speaking, I don't write romantic fiction, but as the RNA embraces 'a wide church', and my novels always include a very intense and complicated love story, I'm a very welcome member. Whilst they only take full membership from mainstream published authors they're also very happy for unpublished authors to join their *New Writers' Scheme,* and welcome them to attend all events. The purpose of the *New Writers' Scheme* is to critique your completed novel, and give serious advice on the chances of getting it published. If your reviewer thinks positively they may pass it to a literary agent for assessment, but if it's 'not quite there' they'll suggest changes to help improve it. If your submission is eventually published mainstream you'll be eligible for *The Joan Hessayon Award*, for which *The Crowded Bed*, was entered in 2007. I didn't win, but it was a great night, and I felt like a 'real author' for the first time. See the website for full details.

Part Twelve:

Reflection

Chapter 19 : What is Success?

Evaluating Success

Success in publishing takes many forms. For a mainstream author it usually means their reviews are good, and their sales figures are enough for their publisher to take a second book. However, for a self-published author, success can take many forms, and some of these are examined here.

For many aspiring writers, self-publishing is seen as a hopeful way of getting noticed as a writer, and going on to land that elusive mainstream publishing deal. It's happening more and more, as echoed by *The Bookseller* magazine, which regularly features such victories, but success doesn't necessarily mean a lucrative publishing deal. What about the authors (as previously outlined) who commission a local village history book, never expecting to sell more than a few hundred copies? Finding a commercial publisher is never their goal, but by selling to the local community, and hearing of their pleasure, is reward enough. One poet I know self-publishes his poetry because it's the culmination of his hobby. He doesn't expect to sell many copies, although it's a joy to him when he does, but to him success is emotional. Gina Claye's prose and poetry book on bereavement, *Don't Let Them Tell You How To Grieve*, certainly comes into this category. Gina (www.ginaclaye.co.uk) wrote this book as a response to some profound events in her own life, and is honoured that Cruse, the bereaved association, recommends it. Small bookshops regularly stock it, and Dovegreyreader, the renowned BookBlogger, chose it as one of her 'top five' books for 2008. So you can see there are many reasons why someone might wish to self-publish a stand-alone book, and why not?

Although I consider I've achieved personal success in making great sales with my books, and my life has been enriched and invigorated along the way, I've not (yet!) been lucky enough to really hit what's known as 'the big time'. In the course of compiling this book I heard about many authors who had made the transition from either self-publishing to mainstream, or mainstream to self-publishing. I know that a great many of you will now be weighing up if you try for a mainstream contract, or take the plunge into self-publishing, and in this next section I can only give you my personal thoughts. Please do not let my views influence you in any way, as you must make up your own mind.

Mainstream Publishing:

An active mainstream publisher is really what every author wants, but here is a list of what you must check out *before you, or your literary agent, sign that contract.*

Don't be so flattered that you whirl around with excitement and assume that everything is going to be utterly fantastic. Bold questions are the order of the day. You need assurance that they're totally committed to your project, it's gone through all the 'in-house' selection processes, and the whole company 'loves it'. After all, your blood, sweat, tears, and hours of slog have gone into the production, it's very precious and valuable to you, and they must take the privilege of publishing it seriously. One publisher contracted me to a novel and then dropped a bombshell that their external reader 'didn't like it', quoting very rude comments. The project was immediately dropped, to mutual relief. This pantomime was a huge waste of my time, shattered my confidence with this particular work, and the emotional aspect is still very hard to bear.

You must make sure you have a named contact to liaise with right from the start, and get to know them well. They must be happy to talk to you on the phone with friendly patience, and promptly answer any questions you submit on email. They must tell you exactly what publicity and marketing they will be doing for you, and what you'll be expected to do for yourself. This includes what expenses you'll have to bear.

You must also have good notice as to when the internal editing process will start. Don't be rushed into tight deadlines as this is not professional, and can lead to a flawed manuscript. And yes, dear readers, this has happened to me, and I was very, very upset with the quality of the result. Make sure you know exactly what the printing production method will be; a conventional printing company with a print-run stock, or Print-on-Demand (often used now by smaller publishers). Lightning Source POD productions can be fantastic but, as previously discussed, it can sometimes hamper the efficiency of distribution. If your book will be produced by another POD firm, other than Lighting Source, ask your publisher (before your contract is signed) if you can see samples as I've seen some very ropey, heart-sink productions. Also discuss which wholesalers will handle your book, and what pre-publication publicity it'll get.

If, for any reason, the given publication date is delayed, then you need to know well in advance. With one book I was given a firm publication date and set up a long raft of publicity and marketing strategies, including a High Street launch, interviews, articles, and talks. When the date was put back at very short notice (twice) I had to cancel all events. When it eventually came out, two months late, I failed to resurrect any of my arrangements. Subsequently, this book had very poor sales.

Self-Publishing

I have very little to add to all the advice and guidance I've written about self-publishing, only to say that *Calling All Authors* is self-published.

Here now, is a definitive article from Polly Courtney, a highly successful young author, who first self-published two very successful novels. She did so well she secured a three-book deal with Harper Collins, but at the end of this term she decided that self-publishing was the best deal for her. I'd like to thank Polly for taking the time and the trouble to write about her experiences. Everything she writes is supremely useful, and demonstrates the dynamism required to be successful.

From Self-Publishing, to Mainstream, and Back Again! by Author Polly Courtney

'I never actually set out to be a writer. Having trained as an engineer at Cambridge University and gone into the 'exciting, glamorous world of investment banking', I expected to make a name for myself in finance. It was only when I realised that it was neither exciting nor glamorous, *and* that it was impossible to make a name for myself without selling my soul, that I decided to get out and write a book. For me, the marketing began even before I'd started writing my first book. I knew that in order for a product to sell, it had to have a well-defined audience, and that audience had to be willing to pay. So when I looked at the collection of anecdotes I'd jotted down whilst working in the City, I asked myself some serious questions: Who would want to read about this world? Would they pay to do so? Initially, I had envisaged the book being a non-fiction exposé – a personal account of my time in the bank. But when I thought about my readers I realised that whilst there was a select group of 'city' folk who might relate to my experiences, there was a much larger audience of young, intelligent females across the country who didn't necessarily work in the city but who wanted to read a good story. So I turned the book into a light-hearted novel.

At a very early stage, I started asking around to find out how the 'book world' worked, and it became clear that if I was to get anywhere, I needed representation. So I polished up my first few chapters, submitted them to the most likely looking literary agents in the Writers and Artists Yearbook and waited for the rejection letters to pour in.

Actually, I was pleasantly surprised. I had three agencies interested in representing me, so I picked the one that seemed the most commercial. With my agent's help, I honed *Golden Handcuffs* into something that was less of a cathartic rant and more of a page-turner.

When my novel was submitted to publishers, the reactions were fairly unanimous: the novel was 'superbly' written, but the subject was 'too niche'. The publishers felt that it would only appeal to those who worked in the square mile, and weren't willing to take it on. I suppose I differ from many authors, because the reason I penned the novel was not 'to be a writer' but 'to get a story out there' – and quickly – because I knew that if I didn't get it published soon then someone else would. That's when I looked into self-publishing.

I felt confident that my first book would sell thousands – not hundreds – of copies because of its topical subject and because of the great feedback it had received from test readers. So with Matador as my self-publishing services provider I commissioned a batch of four thousand copies.

Publishing your own book is like running a small business. You should prepare to be utterly consumed in the months running up to the launch – after all, you're in charge of every department:

• Editing: In my case, this consisted of friends who had offered to proofread the novel.
• Design: I took the cover image photo myself with a borrowed camera and then spent hours on Photoshop playing with fonts and shadows, before letting the real designers get to work.
• Marketing and PR: Actually this was just me, but I invented an assistant for times when someone other than the author should have been making the calls.
• Website: I built and maintained a simple but professional-looking site so that right from the start I 'existed' online.
• Administration: I sent countless emails and pre-release copies of the book to journalists and fiction buyers to give the book its best chances on the shelves.

(n.b. from MC. Always check with your publisher or service provider if pre-release, or proof copies, will be available, as so often they are not. Polly was also able to contact fiction buyers, which could prove tricky without insider knowledge.)

At this point, I had a full-time job in a management consultancy, so I wasn't getting much sleep! Marketing is by far the hardest and most time-consuming element of getting a book on the shelves. Unless you have the marketing clout (and budget) of Penguin, and a track record as a best-selling author, you won't sell many copies if you don't make a bit of 'noise'. I started by emailing everyone I knew and asking whether they knew any journalists – 'whatever type'. I diligently followed up every lead, hoping that media folk would know other media folk and that at some point someone would pick up on my story. It's naïve to expect the press to be interested in a book. Books get published all the time, and the coverage is generally confined to the review sections where it's impossible to stand out (and pretty difficult to

183

even appear). So, given that my marketing budget was zero, I did something different. I turned the story behind the book into a feature. Some people might call it spin, but you have to feed journalists with a story that works for them. Fortunately for me, an *Observer* journalist was looking to write an article about the City. I could offer an alternative to the typical 'rich guys, fast cars' story that was so often portrayed. *'My highflying City job was not worth a life of misery'* was a full-page spread in the August bank holiday edition. After that, I was officially 'newsworthy'. My story was covered in the *Evening Standard*, the *FT, Grazia*, the *Daily Express* and the *Daily Mail* – not always with a positive spin, I should add. You have to expect some negative press if you're going to put yourself on a pedestal.

Not all my approaches have worked. For *Golden Handcuffs,* I started off with the notion that some of my target readers were university students considering careers in the city. I contacted editors of student newspapers up and down the country, angling for press and invitations to speak. In some cases I was successful, but taking a day out to speak to a dozen hung-over undergraduates didn't turn out to be cost effective for me – but the same might not be true for a non-fiction writer if the audience is right. I am a great believer in 'buzz'. If you make out that the launch of your book will be the most exciting event of the century, then people will start talking about it and the excitement becomes a self-fulfilling prophecy. I would never launch a book without a huge event for over a hundred people. That way, you can invite press – who will generally turn up if they think other press might be there too – and give something back to the loyal friends who helped and supported you all the way along. And it doesn't have to cost anything if you tell the venue what a big event it will be.

184

My website has been invaluable. These days, everyone needs some sort of online presence and I regularly get asked to appear on TV and radio to comment on subjects that relate to my books – always through journalists who have found my website through Google or other sites.

I went with a different agent for my second novel, *Poles Apart*, because I felt that my writing was being steered too much towards 'chick lit'. My new agent has been extremely good – not least by selling the rights to both books in several languages and by securing a three-book deal with HarperCollins on the basis of a five-page synopsis. The foreign rights sales were assisted by the international press I attained when launching each novel, and the HarperCollins contract was down to a combination of my agent's hard work and the success of my previous two novels. I have also had interest in the film and TV rights to both novels – mainly through producers who have heard the surrounding 'buzz'.

In late 2011, after publishing three novels, I famously walked out on HarperCollins, being frustrated by the 'chick lit' covers assigned to my books. I happily returned to self-publishing and have since re-issued my first two novels, and published a new one, *Feral Youth*; a compelling story set during the London riots and told from the perspective of a disenfranchised 15-year-old girl.

My approach to marketing has been simple (but exhausting): say yes to every opportunity. I respond to every email, return every call, and accept nearly every invitation to speak. I don't always see a direct impact on book sales, but there is always a benefit of sorts: potential for future exposure, practice at appearing on TV, and a chance to get my views heard... Remember, you never know who might be listening or watching or reading.'

www.pollycourtney.com

Golden Handcuffs (Matador 2007 – re-issued Troubador 2103)

Poles Apart (Matador 2008 – re-issued Troubador 2013)

The Day I Died (Avon 2009)

The Fame (Avon 2010

It's a Man's World (Avon 2011)

*Feral Youth (*Matador 2013)

And finally . . . .

At this stage I'm sure I have no need to say how tough and complicated the publishing industry is. Whatever stage of your journey you're at, I hope that *Calling All Authors* has given you the information and insight you've been seeking. For those of you who already have your book 'in your hands' I also hope you now have the knowledge and inspiration to get out there in the market place and sell it! For the (as yet!) unpublished, maybe you now have enough confidence to make a decision about which way to go.

Good luck to you all, and if you have any feedback, or tales of success, please *do* let me know at mary.cavanagh20@gmail.com

Mary Cavanagh Oxford 2015

The Addendum

The previous version of this book contained endless pages of 'useful contacts' but in looking at them again, five years on, I've decided not to provide a huge list this time. Most of them have proved to be either useless to self-promotion, expensive, or 'publicising' businesses looking for your money. Therefore, I've just included the contributing authors I've mentioned in various categories, useful websites and contacts, and the professional societies who are part of the established book trade.

As ever, with any alien online contact, no matter who has endorsed it, or recommended it, always use your discretion before handing over payment or personal details, without fully satisfying yourself that you're 100% happy with the arrangement.

Calling All Authors
Contributors And Useful Contacts

Contributors
Mary Cavanagh's website: http/:marycavanagh.com
(including blog)
Mary Cavanagh's email: mary.cavanagh20@gmail.com
Andy Severn, director of Oxford eBooks:
www.oxford-ebooks.com
Angela Cecil Reid: www.angelacecilreid.com
Polly Courtney: http://pollycourtney.com
Caro Fraser, novelist: www.caro-fraser.com
Alice Jolly: www.alicejolly.com
John Kitchen: www.johnkitchenauthor.com
Marissa de Luna:
http://the coffeestained manuscript.blogspot.com
Debrah Martin: www.debrahmartin.co.uk
Tim Stevens: http://timstevensblog.wordpress.com
New Generation Publishing:
www.newgeneration-publishing.com

Review Ideas
http://jaffareadstoo.blogspot.co.uk
www.goodreads.com
www.readinggroups.org
www.meetup.com

Bookshops
www.localbookshops.co.uk.

Direct Submission Publishers
www.accentpress.co.uk
www.almabooks.com
www.canongate.tv

www.choc-lit.com
www.legendtimesgroup.co.uk
www.myrmidonbooks.com
www.claretpress.com.
www.honno.co.uk
www.serenbooks.com

Authors Writing Support websites:
www.writewords.org.uk
www.youwriteon.com
www.authonomy.com

Manuscript Assessment Companies
www.theoxfordeditors.co.uk
www.oxfordwriters.com
www.writersworkshop.co.uk
http://literaryconsultancy.co.uk

Authors Help Magazines
www.newbooksmag.com
www.selfpublishingmagazine.co.uk
www.writersnews.co.uk
www.writers-forum.com
www.mslexia.co.uk
www.thebookseller.com
www.selfpublishingreview.com
www.writemag.com
www.writers-online.co.uk
www.writers-forum.com

Stock Photograph Agencies
www.alamy.com
www.fotosearch.com
www.bigstockphoto.com
www.istockphoto.com

The Wholesalers

www.bertrams.com
www.gardners.com
www.granthambookservices.co.uk
www.marston.co.uk
www.orcabookservices.co.uk
www.thebookservice.co.uk (TBS)

Online Platforms

www.facebook.com
https:twitter.com
www.uk.linkedin.com

Sales on Amazon

http://advantage.amazon.co.uk
http://services.amazon.co.uk

ISBN / Bibliographic data

www.isbn.nielsenbookdata.co.uk
www.bowker.co.uk
www.bic.org.uk/8/children's books

Libraries/PLR

kpublib.html
www.plr.uk.com
http://dspace.dial.pipex.com/town/square/ac940/u

Book Groups

www.bookgroup.info
www.thereadinggrouponline.co.uk
www.meetup.com/cities/gb

Literary Festivals
www.britishcouncil.org/arts-literature-literary-
festivals.htm

Authors' Associations
www.rna-uk.org
www.thecwa.co.uk

Miscellaneous/General Interest Sites
www.book2book.co.uk
www.thewordcloud.org
http://authorselectric.blogspot.com
www.stand-store.co.uk
www.google.co.uk/alerts
http://unbound.co.uk

Lightning Source UK Ltd.
Milton Keynes UK
UKOW04f0156271015
261461UK00002B/22/P